The Birth of Prehistoric Chronology

NEW STUDIES IN ARCHAEOLOGY

Series editors
Colin Renfrew, *University of Cambridge*
Jeremy Sabloff, *University of Pittsburgh*

Other titles in the series

Ian Hodder and Clive Orton: *Spatial Analysis in Archaeology*
Keith Muckelroy: *Maritime Archaeology*
Graham Connah: *Three Thousand Years in Africa*
Richard E. Blanton, Stephen A. Kowalewski, Gary Feinman and Jill Appel: *Ancient Mesoamerica*
Stephen Plog: *Stylistic Variation in Prehistoric Ceramics*
Peter Wells: *Culture Contact and Culture Change*
Ian Hodder: *Symbols in Action*
Patrick Vinton Kirch: *Evolution of the Polynesian Chiefdoms*
Dean Arnold: *Ceramic Theory and Cultural Process*
Geoffrey W. Conrad and Arthur A. Demarest: *Religion and Empire: The Dynamics of Aztec and Inca Expansionism*
Graeme Barker: *Prehistoric Farming in Europe*
Daniel Miller: *Artefacts as Categories*
Robin Torrence: *Production and Exchange of Stone Tools*
Rosalind Hunter-Anderson: *Prehistoric Adaptation in the American Southwest*
Michael Shanks and Christopher Tilley: *Re-Constructing Archaeology: Theory and Practice*
Ian Morris: *Burial and Ancient Society: The Rise of the Greek City State*
John Fox: *Maya Postclassic State Formation*

BO GRÄSLUND

The Birth of
Prehistoric Chronology

Dating methods and dating systems
in nineteenth-century Scandinavian archaeology

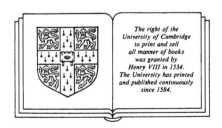

The right of the
University of Cambridge
to print and sell
all manner of books
was granted by
Henry VIII in 1534.
The University has printed
and published continuously
since 1584.

Cambridge University Press

Cambridge
New York   New Rochelle   Melbourne   Sydney

CAMBRIDGE UNIVERSITY PRESS
Cambridge, New York, Melbourne, Madrid, Cape Town, Singapore, São Paulo, Delhi

Cambridge University Press
The Edinburgh Building, Cambridge CB2 8RU, UK

Published in the United States of America by Cambridge University Press, New York

www.cambridge.org
Information on this title: www.cambridge.org/9780521103886

First published 1987
This digitally printed version 2009

A catalogue record for this publication is available from the British Library

Library of Congress Cataloguing in Publication data
Gräslund, Bo.
The birth of prehistoric chronology
(New studies in archaeology)
Bibliography.
Includes index.
1. Archaeological dating – Scandinavia – History – 19th century.
2. Scandinavia – Antiquities.
3. Archaeology – Scandinavia – History – 19th century.
4. Anthropology, Prehistoric – Scandinavia – History – 19th century.
I. Title. II. Series.
CC78.G72 1987   936.3   87–665

ISBN 978-0-521-32249-2 hardback
ISBN 978-0-521-10388-6 paperback

CONTENTS

List of figures and tables vii
Acknowledgements ix

1 **Introduction** 1

2 **The conceptual framework** 5
Conceptual basis 5
Grouping type-analogy 6
Grading type-analogy 6
The find-combination method 7
Stratigraphy 10
Quantitative methods 10

3 **The museum background** 13

4 **C. J. Thomsen and the Three-Age System** 17
Guide to Northern Archaeology 20

5 **The works of Magnus Bruzelius** 31

6 **The Stone Age: the division into two and three periods** 34
The kitchen middens 34
Palaeolithic, Mesolithic and Neolithic 38

7 **The Bronze Age: the division into two periods** 40
The appearance of descriptive typology 44

8 **The Iron Age: the division into two and three periods** 48
The Roman Iron Age 48
The middle Iron Age 51

9 **The pre-Roman Iron Age** 56
The early Iron Age on Bornholm 57
Descriptive typology again 59

10 **The Roman Iron Age: the division into two periods** 62

11 **Coins and Iron Age chronology** 66

12 Dating in the Bronze Age with special reference to Scandinavia 70
The material used 71
Find-combination chronology 76
General evidence of the finds 76
Other evidence 80
Summary of dating evidence and method 81

13 Montelius' own account of his chronological method 86

14 The origin of typology as chronological method 91
The early typological works of Hildebrand and Montelius 91
The originator of classical typology 96
Two terms 'type' and 'typology' 97
Typology and numismatics 99
Typology and Darwinism 101
The typological language 107

15 General aspects 113

Biographical notes 118
References 121
Index 132

FIGURES AND TABLES

Figures

1   Schematic figure of finds with different type content   7
2   Groups of finds with different type contents   7
3   Curves showing the production and consumption of subsequent types   8
4   Find combinations with overlapping type contents   9
5   Two groups of find combinations, establishing a chronological sequence   9
6   Frequency seriation illustrated by cumulative diagram   11
7   Frequency seriation illustrated by a battleship diagram   11
8   C. J. Thomsen. Drawing. Photograph, The National Museum, Copenhagen   13
9   F. Lisch. Drawing. Photograph, Royal Academy of Letters History and Antiquities, Stockholm   18
10   L. Lindenschmit. Photograph, Royal Academy of Letters History and Antiquities, Stockholm   19
11   F. Danneil. Photograph, Royal Academy of Letters History and Antiquities, Stockholm   19
12   Title-page of the Danish edition of Thomsen's *Guide*   22
13   C. J. Thomsen demonstrating his museum. Drawing. Photograph, The National Museum, Copenhagen   25
14   C. J. Thomsen. Drawing. Photograph, The Royal Library, Copenhagen   26
15   S. Nilsson. Photograph, Royal Academy of Letters History and Antiquities, Stockholm   28
16   J. J. A. Worsaae. Photograph, The Royal Library, Copenhagen   35
17   J. Steenstrup. Drawing. Photograph, The Royal Library, Copenhagen   37
18   N. G. Bruzelius. Photograph, University Library, Lund   41
19   V. Boye. Photograph, Royal Academy of Letters History and Antiquities, Stockholm   42
20   J. J. A. Worsaae. Drawing. Photograph, The National Museum, Copenhagen   45
21   C. F. Herbst. Photograph, The Royal Library, Copenhagen   50
22–23   Objects from the bog finds from Torsbjerg and Vimose   52–3
24   C. Engelhardt. Painting. Photograph, The Royal Library, Copenhagen   54
25   E. Vedel. Drawing. Photograph, The Royal Library, Copenhagen   58
26   S. Müller. Photograph, The Royal Library, Copenhagen   63
27   B. E. Hildebrand. Photograph, Royal Academy of Letters History and Antiquities, Stockholm   67
28   O. Montelius. Photograph, University Library, Uppsala   70

29   S. Müller. Photograph, The Royal Library, Copenhagen   72
30   Grid diagrams for periods 2 and 5 of the Bronze Age   75
31   Chronologically mixed finds   78
32   Occurrence diagram of mixed finds   79
33   Artefact types of periods 2 and 5 of the Bronze Age   82
34   H. Hildebrand. Photograph, University Library, Uppsala   92
35   O. Montelius. Photograph, Royal Academy of Letters History and Antiquities, Stockholm   95
36   H. Hildebrand. Photograph, Royal Academy of Letters History and Antiquities, Stockholm   104

Tables

1   Items attributed to the Stone Age, the Bronze Age and the Iron Age, in C. J. Thomsen's *Guide*   21
2   Number of types and find combinations in each of the Bronze Age periods, according to Montelius' *Dating in the Bronze Age*   73
3   Number of find combinations per type in each of the Bronze Age periods, according to Montelius' *Dating in the Bronze Age*   73

ACKNOWLEDGEMENTS

I would like to thank all those who have helped me during the writing and production of this book.

Most of the translation was carried out by Neil Tomkinson, and parts of it by Jacqueline Taffinder. The Berit Wallenberg Foundation has generously given financial support for the translation work. Drawings were redrawn by Alicja Grenberger and Britta Eriksson.

I dedicate this book with admiration to those early scholars in many countries who first laid the basis of prehistoric archaeology as a discipline.

1

Introduction

An increasing interest in the history of archaeological research has been observed in many countries. This phenomenon is a manifestation of the growing methodological awareness amongst archaeologists in general and recognition that such insight can yield valuable perspectives on research carried out in our own time. However, in spite of the appearance of general surveys and many special studies, the history of archaeology remains a neglected field of research. Many important problems still await treatment, not least those concerning questions of methodology in early work on prehistory.

In 1974 I published in Swedish a book entitled *Relative Dating: Chronological Methods in Scandinavian Archaeology*[1] in which I made an analysis of the structure and dating premises of the non-scientific chronological methods used in archaeology.[2] In my opinion, these aspects cannot be ignored in a study of the emergence of the chronological methods and will be referred to in chapter 2, *The conceptual framework*. However, the book also included a study of the development of chronology in Scandinavian archaeology during the nineteenth century which is presented here in a largely revised form.

I have not produced an all-inclusive history of archaeological research in the Nordic area. For a general survey, reference may be made to Ole Klindt-Jensen's book *A History of Scandinavian Archaeology* (1975).[3] My aim is primarily to illustrate a more limited but all the more important aspect, namely the gradual growth and development of the chronological systems and methods during the nineteenth century, from the emergence of C. J. Thomsen's Three-Age System up to the completion of Montelius' Bronze Age chronology in 1885.

Owing to favourable circumstances, archaeological research in Scandinavia was, for a large part of the nineteenth century, methodologically in advance of its time. This applies especially to chronological research. In judging the contribution made by Scandinavian archaeology in this field, emphasis has, first and foremost, been placed on the development of the typological method. Without doubt, the emergence of typology as a dating method has greatly influenced archaeology as a whole, in a positive as well as a negative sense. In this book I will try to explain that the development of this concept and method was preceded by and closely connected with the construction of a chronological framework primarily through the evidence provided by the finds.

In my opinion, the most important contribution of Scandinavian archaeology to the development of chronological methods was not typology as a means of dating, but the early understanding of careful observations of the find contexts in combination with the development of a closer type analysis and type classification. The gradual refinement of

1

the chronological analysis of find observations was by far the most important achievement: the very basis of the development of archaeology from a speculative antiquarianism to a sound science. This elementary stage of archaeology during the first half and the middle of the nineteenth century was the basic premiss not only for the realization of the potentials of typology as an independent method of dating, but also for modern chronology, including physical dating methods. It seems that this fact has been too much obscured in most writings on the history of archaeology.

During the nineteenth century Scandinavian archaeology exerted a significant and growing influence on European antiquarianism and archaeological work. This was made possible not least by an informal system of contacts, communication by letter and personal meetings on journeys. From the middle of the century the academic communication system was gradually extended, primarily by the establishment of international congresses and symposia. Although printed literature is a natural medium for the diffusion of scientific ideas, the number of works by Scandinavian archaeologists available to an international public in translation was strikingly low. European colleagues simply could not read most of the work written by Scandinavian archaeologists in the nineteenth century. Even today, most modern reviews of archaeological history present brief glimpses only of the development of Scandinavian archaeology during this period. The few translations which were produced usually contained general, summarized surveys. Printed congress reports mainly presented results but rarely described how the result was achieved. Primary research reports were virtually never published in foreign languages. Although the non-Scandinavian reader could gain an idea of the level of knowledge in Scandinavian research and of current explanation models, these translated studies afforded limited insight into the analytical methods in Scandinavian archaeology, unless you were very observant. In this connection the considerable time-lag of publication in foreign languages must also be mentioned. The publication of C. J. Thomsen's famous *Guide to Northern Archaeology* took a long time even in Danish, and it did not appear in English until 13 years later. Worsaae's *Primeval Antiquities* was published six years after the original publication and Nilsson's *Primitive Inhabitants* after 25 years.

It may be stating the obvious that all research is a product of its own period and that every researcher bases his work on and progresses from the experience and knowledge of his predecessor. Nevertheless, this is an aspect we tend to ignore when we assess our own research; above all, this attitude often reflects a lack of understanding for the scientific conditions under which the archaeologists of previous generations worked. We have no right to pass judgment on a scientific achievement without relating it to the situation of its own time.

Today chronological work plays an insignificant role in archaeological research. Problems more directly associated with the real aims of archaeology are favoured instead. This is a great step forward, but many modern archaeologists have, as a consequence, almost completely lost the ability to execute a sophisticated chronological analysis on purely archaeological grounds. It is also easy to forget that the chronological work of the scholars of earlier generations forms the platform without which archaeology could not have developed into a real social and humanistic science. What is more, the chronological arrangement of the archaeological material which we now take for granted is not very old. The early antiquarians were not able to draw correct historical conclusions because of a lack of chronological facts. Therefore, the most important task of the early archaeologists was to create, from an original chaos, a reliable chronological division of the archaeological sources. For them, dating was a necessity, never an end in itself. This latter phenomenon belongs mainly to the first half of the twentieth century.

It is true that our chronological knowledge has been increased and differentiated since the last century, but seldom because of revisions which have radically transformed the old systems. In the main, it has been a slow and gradual process of consolidation, in which further fine graduations and adjustments have been made within existing frameworks. The chronological systems which were constructed for the metal ages in Scandinavia during the nineteenth century form the skeleton of those still in use today. This is especially valid for the Bronze Age. No other major chronological work in the whole of the archaeological literature has lasted as well as Oscar Montelius' *Dating in the Bronze Age* (1885).[4] For a century Montelius' detailed chronology of the Scandinavian Bronze Age has been confirmed by new finds. On the whole, this is also the case with the Iron Age chronology. The results were not fixed with the same precision and certainty, but, broadly speaking, the chronological groundwork for the Iron Age was completed with the publication in 1895–7 of Montelius' book *The Chronology of the Scandinavian Iron Age*.[5]

It seems essential that modern archaeologists who use these chronological systems almost every day or insert new material into them should have some knowledge of how they were originally formed. Discussions of theoretical methodology are sometimes also fuelled by hazy ideas about the development of the dating methods. Therefore, greater enlightenment regarding the development of the dating methods and the chronological systems may increase our understanding of questions of chronological method.

One basic point in such an investigation is to try to distinguish the relative contributions made by the different dating methods. How significant were the observations based on the find circumstances? What part was played by pure evolutionary typology? How important were the historical records for the chronological division? How were absolute dates achieved and what was the relationship between relative and absolute dating? The concept of typology has always occupied a central position in discussions of chronological method. It therefore seems justifiable to try to ascertain how the method developed and how the scholars who introduced typology as a means of relative dating applied the method themselves and what meaning they attached to the concept.

However, even if we can, in theory, demarcate evolutionary typology from, for instance, the find combination method, these two methods share certain basic elements which may make it difficult to distinguish between them in practical work. This is because every dating method, whatever its starting-point, includes an element of analogy, without which no results of universal validity can be achieved. It may therefore be hard to define the proportions of the various dating premises in the chronological argumentation, especially in the case of early research literature with its inadequate reports.

The main source for an investigation of this kind is scientific literature which presents the information directly or indirectly. One problem is that in the early literature different operations, such as the reporting of the material or the analysis and presentation of results, are often inseparably interwoven. It was (and still is) fairly common for chronological results to be presented in the form of complete period divisions, chronological sequences or typological series without the methodological procedures being explained. In such cases, it may be difficult or even impossible to shed full light on the methods actually used to carry out the chronological analysis. However, it would seem possible to follow the developments in their essential features.

Another source of information consists of statements by various archaeologists of methodological principles, whether they are concerned with concrete examples or are of a general nature. However, this material requires critical scrutiny and cautious use. Some scholars' accounts of their procedures obviously conflict with the results yielded by an analysis of their works. Such information requires the verification of independent sources in order to be accepted as evidence. The material also includes unprinted preparatory works, correspondence, autobiographical material, contemporary biographical notices, etc.

If we consider the immense advances which were made in archaeological research during the nineteenth century and its considerable volume, the extremely small number of active scholars who carried out the work is striking. It would seem to be the reason why methodological improvements made in respect of a particular period of time were, as a rule, rapidly put into general circulation: archaeologists were few and productive and the leading archaeologists did not specialize to any great extent, but worked over the whole chronological scale and the entire archaeological field.

NOTES

1 Gräslund 1974.
2 Gräslund 1976a and 1976b.
3 Klindt-Jensen 1975. Cf. Kristiansen 1978.
4 Montelius 1885a.
5 Montelius 1895–7.

2

The conceptual framework

The traditional, often routinely employed, terminology for chronological method has proved to be inadequate as a means of analysing chronological arguments. I have therefore prepared a special conceptual apparatus, which I shall briefly present below. I have found it useful in analysing the chronological works of the nineteenth century.[1] In addition, an analytical instrument of this kind may also help to identify methods and appraise them. This is not entirely unimportant, as many archaeologists are innocent when it comes to understanding the basic premises of the dating methods they use. To avoid disturbing readers who are not over-fond of conceptual discussions it has, however, been given a rather obscure place in the book as a whole. Needless to say, this book deals only with purely archaeological, non-scientific dating methods.

As a starting-point, I wish to call attention to the use of the term *typology*. It is seldom clear what archaeologists mean precisely by this term, and there is no unambiguous definition which one can claim to be generally accepted. Typology is, especially in Scandinavia, used to mean an evolutionistic *gradation of types* according to similarity, but typology is also used to denote the process of *type classification*. But the term typology is also used to denote the *result* of either of these procedures or *any classification* whatever the method behind it.[2] In short, typology is used to stand for practically every conceivable analysis of similarities and classification.

A term with such an extensive meaning is unusable as an analytical instrument. A clear demarcation between basic methods and procedures within methods seems necessary. The fact that chronological research in practice often consists of a complicated interaction between different kinds of analogies calls for a differentiation of the terminology. In order to understand the distinctions between them, the basic procedures then have to be analysed in their purest form.

Conceptual basis
The first prerequisite is to distinguish between the *grouping* and the *grading* dating procedures.

As archaeological dating often is a complicated process, the terminology should have a certain amount of flexibility. The present terminology has therefore been adapted to two main, independent principles of classification, based on different chronological premisses.

The two poles consist of

(a) *type analogy* based on the comparison of the *physical properties* of the artefacts, and

(b) *find analogy* based on the *spatial relations* of the artefacts.

Furthermore, it is necessary to have a conceptual instrument which describes the different stages in all conceivable dating methods. For the purposes of structuring, I have chosen the following main concepts for all grouping methods:

(a) Type-forming analogy
(b) Horizoning type-analogy
(c) Contrasting type analogy

These terms and concepts together serve as an instrument for giving a general description of the operations associated with the basic, chronological methods. At the same time, they tell us something about the product which they have resulted in.

Grouping type-analogy

The grouping dating procedures can thus be roughly differentiated in the following three groups.

(a) *Type-forming analogy*. The procedure of bringing together artefacts or other units to form types on the basis of comparisons with regard to similarity and dissimilarity. Whether pronounced or not, type affinity is considered to often reflect chronological affinity. Type formation is the primary and fundamental stage in *all* general, chronological analyses.
(b) Horizoning type-analogy simply means a more systematic kind of type formation than the former, which produces a type with a certain quantitative range, so that it is regarded as a type horizon and a time horizon.
(c) *Contrasting type-analogy* means the contrasting of types and type horizons on the basis of dissimilarity and concluding from this that they are *not* contemporaneous.

(a), (b) and (c) together represent the *grouping type-analogy*. They represent chiefly differences of degree. Thus, the contrasting procedure presupposes the occurrence of at least two different type horizons, and the horizoning procedure in its turn involves a quantitative widening or systematization of the type-forming procedure. The collective term grouping type-analogy expresses the chronological premiss of all three procedures – the bringing together of artefacts to form types and type groups. Thus, grouping type-analogy includes all forms of archaeological classification and, consequently, all kinds of archaeological dating.

Grading type-analogy

This means the procedure of arranging artefacts, chiefly types, according to their degrees of similarity and dissimilarity, in what is assumed to be a causally coherent sequence, which is interpreted as an unbroken, chronological order. The grading type-analogy is always preceded by an element of grouping type-analogy.

Grading type-analogy comprises typology in the sense of the classical, Scandinavian, development typology. It includes related procedures, such as the seriation of types unsupported by collective finds, i.e. development seriation or form seriation. It embraces this concept as a whole, irrespective of whether or not premises in the form of development theories or the like are referred to and irrespective of how simple or complicated the operations are.

The find-combination method

The term find-combination method should, properly, have been 'find-analogy method'. However, 'find-combination method' is strongly entrenched in Nordic archaeology and, as there is no real disagreement as to its meaning, there is no reason to abandon it.

I here give the concept find combination a relatively broad meaning, not confined only to closed finds in the form of grave or depot finds. Every find which is *used* as a chronological unit is counted as a find combination, irrespective of how wide its chronological span is. It is usual to distinguish between two kinds of collective finds – closed finds and accumulated finds.

A *closed find* is interpreted as having come into existence on one and the same occasion. Thus, in a closed find the artefacts are assumed to have been deposited absolutely simultaneously. Closed finds are chiefly grave finds, but sacrificial and depot finds and hoards may also be closed finds.

An *accumulated find* has been formed by accumulation over varying periods of time and has some common, spatial framework. Thus, the chronological affinity within an accumulated find is not contemporaneous in the strict sense but a relative chronological affinity. Here we are concerned chiefly with settlement finds and other gradually accumulated finds, for example, many sacrificial finds and stratigraphically demarcated units within these finds.

A dwelling-site, for example, may be reckoned as a find combination in a chronological sense, regardless of what its chronological span may be. This question is decided entirely by the purpose of the investigation and of the nature of the source material. Finds originating from periods and societies in which cultural changes took place at a

			A + B + C	D + E + F	G + H + J
			A + B + C	D + E + F	G + H + J
			A + B + C	D + E + F	G + H + J
			A + B + C	D + E + F	G + H + J
A + B + C	D + E + F	G + H + J	A + B + C	D + E + F	G + H + J

Fig. 1. Three finds with different type contexts. A *single* series like this proves very little from a chronological point of view.

Fig. 2. Groups of finds with different type contexts. Archaeological types are seldom completely arbitrary but reflect some common norms in prehistoric society (stylistic, functional, social, etc.). As prehistoric types were generally produced over a certain period of time many closed finds contain artefacts of about the same types, which are from the same 'periods'. Repeated finds of this kind help to establish type and find horizons, but they cannot without additional information be used to create chronological sequences.

slow rate naturally allow us to assume a greater chronological span in the finds than those in which development proceeded more rapidly. In other words, the question of the find-combination concepts is also the question of whether a find is used as a find combination or not.

In order that the chronological affinity of a find may be used for chronological purposes and brought out onto a wider plane, a comparison must be made between artefacts in the find and other artefacts. In other words, a type analysis must be carried out in accordance with the grouping-type-analogy procedure.

Owing to the fact that archaeological types always have a certain, varying period of manufacture and use, the closed finds will often consist of types of somewhat different ages. In many of the closed finds, some or all of the artefacts may have been used for varying periods before they were buried together. Such a find thus links together types of different ages, making it possible to arrange them in continuous, vertical time-scales, i.e. in a relative-chronological system, according to the chain-link principle. This possibility would be very limited if every find contained artefacts used for exactly the same period of time. What is needed is an adequate number of finds with chronologically slightly mixed contents, so that groups of finds which, through a grouping type-analogy, have been brought together to time horizons can be linked together in vertical order. Consequently, the limiting weakness of the find-combination method, the inner time-span of finds, is at the same time the foundation and prerequisite of the method. In my experience, many archaeologists, including experienced and skilful chronologists, lack a clear understanding of this fundamental fact.

A sort of chain-link procedure is also used to establish contemporary find horizons. If the investigation is extended to geographically separate, cultural regions, this procedure is often called *cross-dating*.

The following combination procedures can thus be distinguished.

1 *Horizoning, combination method.* The method of bringing out the finds' special chronological affinity, in order to establish time horizons of artefact and find types, with the aid of horizoning type-analogy.
2 *Contrasting, combination method.* The method of bringing about, with the aid of contrasting type-analogy, the chronological content of the find, in order to establish distinctly separate, time horizons of artefact types and find types.

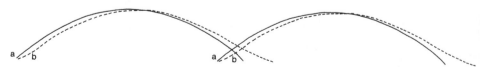

Fig. 3. Schematic curves showing, (a) the production, (b) the consumption of two subsequent types. Utility goods generally had a short life-span. Therefore, the majority of the artefacts of this kind were deposited within the time of production. However, a minor number was always in circulation *after* production had ceased. In addition, the production of one type may also have begun before the production of the preceding type had ended. All this creates opportunities for the appearance of chronologically 'mixed' finds, containing types characteristic of two adjacent 'periods'. Such finds may complicate find combination dating, but they are, at the same time, the main instrument for linking together type horizons into relative chronological sequences (see also fig. 5).

The horizoning and contrasting procedures together form the *grouping combination method*.

3 *Grading combination method.* The procedure of arranging types, on the basis of the different ages of the artefacts within the finds and with the aid of the grouping type-analogy, in continuous time sequence in accordance with the chain-link principle. As for the type-analogy method, distinct and sharp boundaries cannot, as a rule, be drawn in practical work between the horizoning and contrasting stages.

Summary

The terms and concepts for the procedures discussed above can be summarized as follows:

Type-analogy procedure	*Find-combination procedure*
	Type-forming analogy
	(type classification)
Grouping analogy	Grouping, combination method
(a) Horizoning	(a) Horizoning
(b) Contrasting	(b) Contrasting
Grading analogy	Grading, combination method

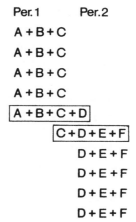

```
1. A+B+ C
2        C +D+ E
3             E +F +G
```

Fig. 4. Three different find combinations connected by artefact types C and E. A *single* series of this kind does not tell us whether this is a chronological sequence from A/B to F/G or whether all the artefacts from A to G are contemporary. Cf. fig. 5.

```
        Per. 1      Per. 2
        A + B + C
        A + B + C
        A + B + C
        A + B + C
        A + B + C + D
              C + D + E + F
              D + E + F
              D + E + F
              D + E + F
              D + E + F
```

Fig. 5. Most find combinations reflect a type of time stabilisation, they are within a 'period'. However, there is, as a rule, a sufficient number of chronologically mixed finds from the transition between the periods (fig. 3) to make a link between the horizons possible. In contrast to the case in fig. 4, the number of finds makes it clear that this is a chronological sequence.

Stratigraphy

Stratigraphic dating is based on the fact that artefacts or other archaeological units have been deposited on top of each other, proving that the uppermost artefacts were deposited later than the underlying ones. On the other hand, the stratification seldom tells us about the span of time involved. Thus, the time difference within a specific layer may well be greater than that between two distinct, adjacent layers.

While the find combination may tell us that the artefacts are absolutely contemporaneous as regards the date when they were deposited, the stratigraphical relation is the opposite. The stratification indicates non-contemporaneousness as regards deposition. The stratification has yet another chronological characteristic: it indicates in principle the chronological *direction* of the units concerned.

It is essential to make these distinctions between stratigraphy and the find-combination method, precisely because the methods are in practice often so intimately interwoven. For, if there are separate layers, either natural or metric, there are also find units which correspond to the concept of find combination. In interpreting and using separate, accumulated layers as chronological *units*, we are also operating in the sphere of the combination method, irrespective of how long a time span the layers represent. This is also what generally happens in archaeological work. We are then faced with a chronological procedure which might be called combination stratigraphy. Stratigraphy in its pure form is in fact a much rarer phenomenon than combination stratigraphy.

In other words, combination stratigraphy makes use in principle of *three* dating components: (1) the absolute non-contemporaneousness of the stratification of the deposition, (2) the information about the *chronological direction*, and (3) the absolute or relative, *chronological affinity* of the find combination.

Stratigraphy is, of course, applied with the aid of type analogy. The chronological value of stratification is therefore also conditioned by the type properties of the artefacts, and is proportional to the degree of type definability of the artefacts.

Thus, all stratigraphy is *directive* as regards chronology. In its pure form, it is *contrasting*. Combination stratigraphy occurs in *contrasting and grading* forms.

Quantitative methods

A detailed conceptual apparatus for the quantitative methods of dating may be left out of consideration here, as these methods largely belong to a later phase of archaeological development than that described in this book.[3] They have been applied particularly to accumulated finds but may, of course, also be applied to closed finds. The basis is the observation of which types which *occur* and *not occur* and *how often* they are found together. We accordingly note the *occurrence and non-occurrence* of the types in the finds, and the *number* of finds in which they are combined with each other. This kind of find-combination analysis involves making an external comparison of the types. It is a complete counterpart to the classical, combination method applied to closed finds, as reflected, for example, in Montelius' Bronze Age chronology of 1885[4] and Flinders Petrie's sequence dating of Predynastic, Egyptian grave material.[5]

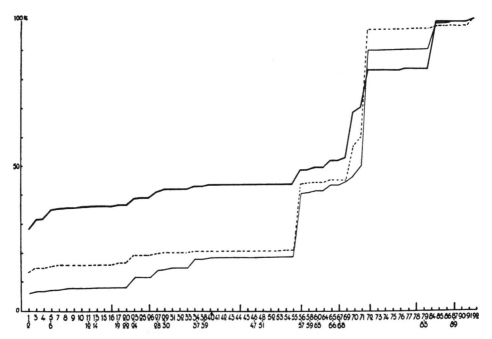

Fig. 6. Cumulative diagram where the curves show the relative frequency of types within each find. The chronological order between the units is obtained by comparing the curves. Cf. fig. 7. (After Bordes 1960.)

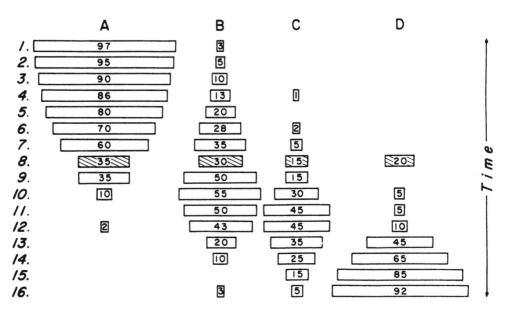

Fig. 7. 'Battleship' diagram. The horizontal rows show the relative frequency of each type with regard to all units. The chronological order between the units is obtained by arranging the rows into figures which are as smooth as possible. Frequency seriation as shown in figs. 6–7 is a special case of the find analogy method. Today, the cultural premisses for frequency seriation as a chronological method can hardly be regarded as tenable. (After Dunnel 1970, fig. 3.)

NOTES

1 Gräslund 1974, 1976a and 1976b.
2 Cf. Klejn 1982, pp. 1ff.
3 Gräslund 1974 and 1976b.
4 Montelius 1885a.
5 Petrie 1901.

3

The museum background

The Scandinavian countries, primarily Denmark and Sweden, played a predominant part in the process which transformed archaeology from the unsystematic collecting of curiosities into a leading science in cultural history. The contributions most discussed were the Three-Age System and typology. In actual fact, the process concerned archaeological method in general and chronological method in particular. Moreover, the Scandinavian countries obtained a comparatively detailed and reliable chronological framework for their prehistoric past at a fairly early date.

It was not a new idea to divide the earliest history of man into epochs according to the level of technological culture. Three-period systems had often been suggested previously. Nevertheless, it was only in the 1820s and 1830s through the agency of C. J. Thomsen in Copenhagen that the Three-Age System could be formulated and applied to a body of material in a definite and convincing fashion. Why? As regards the typological method, it had been similarly foreshadowed by a growing consciousness of a developmental relationship between artefacts or other cultural products. In archaeology, however, these different intellectual currents were first expressed in a deliber-

Fig. 8. Christian Jürgensen Thomsen (1788–1865). Drawing in private possession.

ately arranged, theoretical programme and in clear, practical applications during the 1870s by Hans Hildebrand and Oscar Montelius in Stockholm.

Why did this development take place in the Scandinavian countries? Why not in western or central Europe or somewhere else? Thomsen, Worsaae, Hildebrand, Montelius and Müller were certainly talented men, but did they really represent a greater body of potential talent than was obtainable in other countries? It seems unlikely.

During the first half and the middle of the nineteenth century, the centre of gravity in scientific archaeology in Sweden was Lund. In central Sweden at that time there were no counterparts to archaeologists in Lund such as Magnus Bruzelius, Sven Nilsson or Nils Gustaf Bruzelius, apart from Bror Emil Hildebrand, who received all his basic scientific training in Lund and Copenhagen. It is not difficult to see a connection with the conditions in the museums. In 1805, the Lund collections comprised a much larger number of artefacts than the Stockholm collections did in 1837, when Bror Emil Hildebrand was appointed Chief Custodian of National Antiquities. During the first decades of the nineteenth century, the Lund collections certainly held their own in relation to the Copenhagen Museum. Very large private collections of artefacts – which in some cases were later incorporated into those of the Stockholm Museum – were also available, especially those belonging to Magnus Bruzelius and Sven Nilsson. When Thomsen became secretary of the Antiquities Commission in Copenhagen in 1817 and Hildebrand Chief Custodian in Stockholm 20 years later, a period of tremendous growth began for the two museums. By systematic acquisitions, the Stockholm collections were enlarged at great speed from the 1840s onward, an enlargement which was closely associated with the great land-reclamation works in agriculture and, as time went on, also with more methodical, excavation work. Only from the 1860s onward did the quantitatively and qualitatively stabilized collections in Stockholm produce the first generation of scientific archaeologists, represented by Hans Hildebrand, Oscar Montelius and Hjalmar Stolpe.

In a similar way, the conditions in the museums explained the leading position held by Scandinavian archaeology internationally during the greater part of the nineteenth century. Real *national collections* of archaeological material were established at a comparatively early date. The originally unsystematically assembled collections in Copenhagen and Stockholm were gradually developed into museums which were representative of their national cultural spheres, Denmark and Sweden respectively, and had no counterparts in Europe. Only collections of this kind afforded an overall view of the source material which *made it possible to grasp the general and the typical features* in the confusion of never wholly identical objects, which separately yielded few basic data for chronological or cultural conclusions. This overall survey was favoured by the fact that at that time a much greater proportion of the collections was kept on exhibition than is the case in modern museums. Through their representativeness, these collections especially made it possible for the local variations in source material to be interpreted in the correct perspective.

The endeavours of the Scandinavian archaeologists to form central archaeological collections concealed a clear, scientific aim. Bror Emil Hildebrand and Thomsen have testified to this in their autobiographical memoranda.[1] Thomsen's museum work also reflects his view that a developed system of museums was the prerequisite condition for the healthy development of scientific archaeology.[2]

Worsaae's work and writings are characterized by the same attitude to the scientific collections. His book *Recollections* – written in 1858 but not printed until 1934 – also expresses an awareness of the great scientific advantage which the Copenhagen collections gave Danish archaeology; through 'the excellent material of national antiquities collected by Thomsen and arranged at an earlier date than in any other country in Europe, Denmark had achieved a considerable advantage, which it was a matter of maintaining, and, if possible, extending', he writes.[3] Worsaae, the founder of comparative archaeology *sensu strictu*, also urged the necessity of making a national and international survey of the archaeological source material. This became evident to him during his extensive study trips on the continent and in the British Isles in the middle of the century.[4]

The conditions in the German-speaking countries were particularly striking. Worsaae found that the museum and scientific collections were so disordered that he not only published his views on this subject in an article entitled *National Antiquities in Germany*, but also felt called upon to issue it in German.[5] One of his principal theses here is that scientific archaeology in Germany had been greatly retarded in its development because the museum and antiquities system was divided into a large number of local units, which was, in its turn, a consequence of the great political disunity. On this account, German archaeologists had not succeeded in obtaining the necessary overall survey of the source material. He even considered it likely 'that no German archaeologist *has ex professo* previously had an opportunity to tour Germany, in order to specially examine its collections of national antiquities'. However, he himself had obtained such an overall survey during his tour of the German-speaking countries. He was therefore able to present what he himself rightly emphasized was the first modern survey of Germany's prehistory.[6]

With regard to the slow development of national archaeology in, for example, England, France and the southern parts of central Europe, Worsaae had observed, correctly, that the interest in ancient monuments in these countries was absorbed by their numerous Roman monuments, while the national monuments were neglected. He therefore saw a connection between the early development of archaeology in northern Europe and the fact that this region had never been included in the Roman Empire's sphere of interest. But also, Scandinavia seems to have had a more homogeneous culture in prehistoric times which Worsaae – with good reason in my opinion – regarded as contributory to the advantage enjoyed by the Scandinavian archaeologists. The great cultural disunity in prehistoric times in central Europe, where we have to reckon with a long series of different influxes of population, made the initial position of national archaeology distinctly worse.[7]

Hans Hildebrand had a similar experience 20 years later. He and his father were keen advocates of a central, national collection in Sweden – something which then was by no means an obvious requirement. The idea of a central museum is the predominant message in Hildebrand's pamphlet *Scientific Archaeology, Its Task, Requirements and*

Rights, which appeared at the beginning of 1873, shortly after his return home from his great European tour. In the well-known section in which Hildebrand introduces the term 'typology' into archaeology, he stresses the importance of the central museums for scientific archaeology and for the typological method:

> Only the archaeologist who is working at that stage (i.e. the typological stage) knows how much archaeology needs for its development. People have difficulty in understanding this in Sweden, where we are used to possessing a large museum. Everyone who leaves Scandinavia in order to continue his studies soon learns what it means to try to acquire learning in the small collections. Why has Scandinavian archaeology, generally speaking, an advantage over foreign archaeology, if not because Scandinavian archaeologists have had an opportunity to study in their museums not isolated specimens but whole series and their development? The individual objects in the foreign collections also speak to them, because they know in advance the series in which these objects can be placed, while these objects are mute to most of the foreign scientists.[8]

One cannot better express in a few words the importance of the central collections for the scientific development of early archaeology. There are good grounds for assuming that the national archaeological collections which were comparatively well arranged at an early date in Scandinavia were a strong contributory reason for the leading position of Scandinavian archaeology internationally during the nineteenth century, especially as regards the development of the chronological methods. Mention can be made here of the knowledgeable German scholar Ludwig Lindenschmit who as late as the 1880s was unwilling to accept the idea of a separate Bronze and Iron Age.[9] This hesitation is easier to understand if we bear in mind that, in central Germany, there were few opportunities to examine a large and representative collection of find contexts. It would also appear evident that the early, purposeful advocates of the idea of central museums in Scandinavia – men like Thomsen, Worsaae, B. E. Hildebrand and H. Hildebrand – pursued a museum policy which was characterized by an understanding of the basic needs of scientific archaeology.

NOTES

1 B. E. Hildebrand 1884 (cf. Montelius 1915, pp. 33 and 37), Thomsen 1864.
2 B. Hildebrand 1937–8, pp. 353f., 359ff. and 624f.
3 Worsaae 1934, p. 94; cf. pp. 100f. and 147.
4 Worsaae 1846b, 1884, pp. 171ff., and 1934, pp. 94, 100f., 128ff. and 147.
5 Worsaae 1946b and 1846c.
6 Worsaae 1846b, pp. 126–46; cf. 1934, p. 128.
7 Worsaae 1846b, pp. 117 and 125f.
8 H. Hildebrand 1873a, p. 16; cf. Montelius 1884a, pp. 5ff.
9 Böhner 1981.

4

C. J. Thomsen and the Three-Age System

In 1813 the Dane Vedel Simonsen briefly presented a division of prehistoric time into a stone age, a copper age and an iron age,[1] a division which has sometimes been pointed out as the starting point of his countryman Christian Jürgensen Thomsen's famous Three-Age System. However, Vedel Simonsen's division into three periods was vaguely worded and presented without any kind of argumentation. What is more, even as late as the middle of the century, long after Thomsen's Three-Age System had been generally accepted in Scandinavia, Vedel Simonsen made a statement which suggested that he had scarcely heard of a three-period system.[2] It is clear that his announcement was only an unoriginal repetition of an old, scholastic tradition. It is also significant that Vedel Simonsen himself never in any way claimed to have priority as the creator of the Three-Age System in Denmark.

As we all know, scholars had, ever since classical antiquity, divided cultural history into different stages and periods of time, just as they had during the sixteenth, seventeenth and eighteenth centuries in many quarters of Europe. Many proposals were presented for the division of past time, often in terms of a two or three-period system, with a stone age, a copper or bronze age and an iron age.[3]

This is not particularly surprising. During antiquity, there was a living tradition according to which a bronze age had preceded antiquity's own iron age. The antiquaries of later times knew of this tradition from the writings of the classical authors, just as they knew from the written sources that the technology of the Romans, the Celts and the Germans was based on iron. Naturally, they also knew that this applied to the culture of their own time, that they themselves were living in the prolongation of the iron age. In other words, it was obvious that the iron age represented the last stage in this developmental series.

The discovery of the American continents had also made the Europeans aware of a stage of culture in which metal was unknown and which was based exclusively on stone and organic material. In that case, it must have been very natural to conclude that the many stone tools and weapons which had been found in large numbers all around Europe, with no connection whatever with metal artefacts, had also belonged to a stage of culture in which the use of metal was still unknown. The antiquaries who believed in the occurrence of a separate bronze age (which was not quite so self-evident, as bronze and iron objects were often found together) had scarcely any other choice than to place this bronze age between the stone and the iron ages. If we also bear in mind that, for the observant archaeologist, there were after all a great many find circumstances which supported the hypothesis of a three-period system, we can hardly describe this as exclusively the fruit of learned speculation. The old idea of a three-period system undoubtedly contained a good deal of logic and was, at least in part, based on sound and shrewd reasoning.

It is, accordingly, well known that there were predecessors of Thomsen's Three-Age System with which Thomsen was familiar. Why did none of them gain a foothold in the antiquarian world and why did Thomsen's formulation of the Three-Age System have such penetrative power? The answers to these questions also give the answer to the question of whether the old tradition was of any decisive importance to Thomsen's Three-Age System.

It has long been clear that Thomsen was not only the first archaeologist to formulate and define in a clear and unambiguous manner the Three-Age System but was also the first to publish it, partly by applying it in his own museum work and partly by communicating it on an extensive scale to his colleagues. The vaguer chronological divisions which, for example, the Germans Danneil and Lisch published in 1836 and 1837 respectively,[4] i.e. at practically the same time as the publication of Thomsen's book *Ledetraad til nordisk Oldkyndighed* (1836) (English edition *Guide to Northern Archaeology*, 1848), were not, on account of their incompleteness, fully accepted even in German archaeological research. They are nowadays assigned, even in German historiography, a secondary role as regards the origin and emergence of the Three-Age System.[5] Accordingly our main interest is in the Three-Age System as elaborated by Thomsen.

It is difficult to determine exactly the origin of Thomsen's System. It seems to have matured gradually during the period immediately after 1817, when Thomsen began the work of re-arrangement at the Museum of National Antiquities in Copenhagen. To all appearances, the System began to take shape as early as 1818 and was complete about

Fig. 9. Friedrich Lisch (1801–83), German prehistorian.

1824–5.[6] In other words, it was published in exhibition form more than 10 years before it appeared in print in the famous *Guide* in 1836. As a matter of fact, it was applied in museum exhibitions also in Sweden and Norway several years before publication of the *Guide* owing to Thomsen's extensive scientific and personal connections. As early as 1830, Bror Emil Hildebrand arranged, in consultation with Thomsen and in accordance with Thomsen's intentions, the archaeological collections in the Historical Museum at

Fig. 10. Ludwig Lindenschmit (1809–93), German prehistorian.

Fig. 11. Friedrich Danneil (1783–1868), German prehistorian.

Lund University on the basis of the Three-Age System. Hildebrand also attempted to apply the same principles in the Stockholm museum, first in connection with a short commission in 1831 and then after his appointment there in 1833. However, he was unable to complete his plans until he had been appointed Chief Custodian and head of the museum in 1837.[7] In Norway, Rudolf Keyser applied the Three-Age System in the museum at Christiania (Oslo), probably in 1833 and at the latest in 1835.[8] When *Ledetraad* was finally published, the Three-Age System was already generally known and accepted in the leading archaeological circles in Scandinavia.

Guide to Northern Archaeology

Guide to Northern Archaeology appeared as a guide to the collections of the Museum of National Antiquities in Copenhagen. Apart from the introductory chapter on Old Norse literature, the whole book was written by Thomsen. In the parts which deal with prehistory, he discusses, in turn, the ancient remains, the types of artefacts, the chronological division, the runes and the coins, and concludes with a short guide to the technique of archaeological investigation.[9]

The actual arguments in favour of the Three-Age System do not occupy a prominent place in the *Guide*, which, like other works by Thomsen, has the character of sober accounts of research results, in which the scientific argumentation is given indirectly or in passing. However, this work yields far more to the reader than the statement that prehistory can be divided into three consecutive periods, represented by the raw materials stone, bronze and iron.

The important restriction that Thomsen defined the metal ages primarily on the basis of the cutting weapons and tools is well known.[10] However, the description of the various ages, the ancient remains and the artefact groups yields several other items of information that are interesting as regards the evaluation of the grounds on which Thomsen constructed his chronological system. A number of such items have been brought together in table 1.

As the Three-Age System is a division defined by, *inter alia*, technological criteria, i.e. the tool material, it has often been interpreted, especially in non-Scandinavian literature, as a purely theoretical model, a working hypothesis emanating from Thomsen's need to have at hand a simple and practical principle for the arrangement of museum material. Sometimes it has also been described as a technological model.[11] Accordingly, the empirical element would have been restricted to the frequent handling of the objects in the museum, and the real proof of the correctness of the Three-Age System is generally ascribed to field observations made by Worsaae afterwards. However, a close examination of *Ledetraad* and of Thomsen's archaeological work in general will force us to modify this view.

On considering table 1, one is at once struck by the fact that Thomsen succeeded in arranging in chronological order, on the whole correctly, a long series of phenomena, besides artefacts of stone, bronze and iron. How was he able to do this? One's immediate impression is that it is impossible to incorporate all these datings naturally into either a hypothesis based on written history or a speculative model of cultural evolution. How could Thomsen know that silver was not used before the Iron Age and that gold was

Table 1. *Some phenomena associated with the Three Ages in* Ledetraad

Categories	Stone Age	Bronze Age	Iron Age
Stone	x		
Bronze		x	x
Iron			x
Copper		x	
Gold		x	x
Silver			x
Amber	x		
Pottery	x	x	x
Glass bowls			x
Glass beads	x	x	x
Bronze lurs		x	
Tutuli		x	
Stone-chamber tombs	x		
Stone-cist graves		x	
Chamber tombs in barrows			x
Uncremated corpses	x	x	x
Cremated corpses		x	x
Cinerary-urn graves with awls, tweezers and knives (= razors)		x	
Horse buried in grave			x

used not only during the Iron Age but also during the Bronze Age and even a little during the Stone Age? How could he know that amber objects dated chiefly from the Stone Age?[12] Furthermore, how could he know that pottery was made during all three ages? What made him think that glass beads occurred long before the Iron Age, when at the same time he knew that glass beakers dated only from the Iron Age?[13] There are no reasonable answers to these questions, except that this is precisely what the find circumstances show.

The impression that observations regarding the find associations were the crucial starting-point when Thomsen formulated his Three-Age System is strengthened by his definition of the Iron Age as the period when the *cutting* weapons and tools were made of iron. This idea appears to be quite foreign to anyone who sets out from an idea of cultural evolution. Precisely the fact that bronze and iron objects were discovered together in the finds had, before Thomsen, been an insuperable obstacle to a division of European prehistory into periods based on the belief in cultural evolution. However, owing to his collected observations of a large number of finds, Thomsen was able to establish that it was the cutting tools made of iron that defined the Iron Age.

The same impression is given by Thomsen's information about burial customs and grave types: stone-chamber tombs containing uncremated corpses date from the Stone Age, stone cists containing uncremated and especially cremated corpses but also cinerary-urn graves containing the find constellation of tweezers, awl and knife

(= razor) date from the Bronze Age, and both uncremated and cremated corpses, timbered burial chambers under barrows and sometimes horses among the burial finds date from the Iron Age. Here, a careful observer's experience of the find associations clearly tells. Bronze lurs and tutuli are among the few types of artefacts of the non-cutting kind which Thomsen dates, quite correctly, to the Bronze Age. He does so explicitly, with direct reference to the fact that they were found together with other objects which can be assigned to the Bronze Age (swords, as far as the lurs are concerned).[14]

It seems obvious to me that here we are a long way from any simple, evolutionary model and that Thomsen's Three-Age System must be primarily regarded as a *chronological* system, which was based in all essentials on observations of the find associations. In this connection, the three main periods – the Stone, Bronze and Iron Ages – were distinguished by the *grouping, find-combination* method.

But what about the relative chronological order of the three ages? Thomsen, of course, knew extremely well that the Iron Age was the final period of prehistory, both from the Old Norse sources and from historical information about the Romans and the Celts.[15] Accordingly, the problem was actually only to order the Stone Age and the Bronze Age in relation to each other. One cannot, of course, wholly disregard the fact that Thomsen was influenced by the early concepts, in which stone was regarded as the material with which man first made tools. Moreover, he himself speaks on one occasion

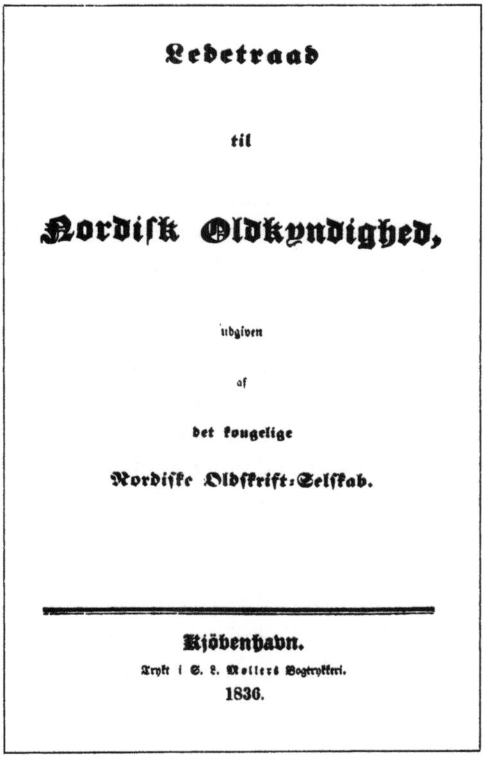

Ledetraad

til

Nordisk Oldkyndighed,

udgiven

af

det kongelige

Nordiske Oldskrift-Selskab.

Kjöbenhavn.

Trykt i S. L. Møllers Bogtrykkeri.

1836.

Fig. 12. The title-page of the famous *Ledetraad* (1836), the Danish edition of the *Guide to Northern Archaeology* (1848), in which Thomsen, for the first time in writing, clearly formulated the Three-Age System.

of the Three-Age System as 'the old idea'.[16] It must, on the whole, have been very natural to think that the Stone Age came before the Bronze Age.

However, we find in the *Guide* also a clear reference to the find associations, as regards the relative order of the Stone and the Bronze Ages, i.e. the reference to *mixed finds*, in which objects made of bronze and gold were sometimes included with the Stone Age finds, for example, in stone-chamber tombs:

> The large stone-chamber tombs seem to have been built about the period when the first metals came, gradually and probably sparingly, into use in Scandinavia. In them, we have, as has already been noted, generally found the corpses uncremated, often with crude urns beside them, very seldom anything of metal, in any case only little bronze or gold and never anything of silver or iron, but almost solely stone artefacts and simple ornaments of amber.[17]

Now, whether it was a question of real mixed finds or finds which had come into existence on account of secondary burials, it is obvious that Thomsen had understood their chronological significance. Even though such finds were few, they would seem to have sufficiently strongly convinced Thomsen of the correctness of the otherwise reasonable supposition that the Stone Age should be placed first in the series. Here, we accordingly have, as regards the relative order of the Stone Age and the Bronze Age, also a clear element of the *grading, find-combination method*.

However, there was yet another, very natural reason why Thomsen should place the Bronze Age after the Stone Age and one which is also directly connected with the find circumstances. I am thinking of his definition of the Iron Age, which must have originated from the observation that bronze objects were generally found together with iron objects. If Thomsen knew from the finds that bronze was used throughout the Iron Age, he could not, of course, have imagined a metal-free, Stone-Age period intercalated between the Bronze and the Iron Ages.

As has been pointed out, we may gather, *inter alia*, from Thomsen's private correspondence the decisive importance which he attached to the find circumstances during the period when he was engaged in re-arranging the collections in the Museum of National Antiquities, i.e. precisely the time when his Three-Age System was taking shape.[18] His attitude was expressed as early as 1821 in a letter to the Swedish historian Schröder, in which he emphasized that 'nothing is more important than to point out that hitherto we have not paid sufficient attention to what was found together'. Similar lines of thought also emerged in letters to Schröder the following year:

> we still do not know enough about most of the antiquities either; whether they date from A.D. 100 or A.D. 900 or even from before the introduction of the worship of Odin into Scandinavia only future archaeologists may be able to decide, but *they will never be able to do so if they do not observe what things are found together* and our collections are not brought to a greater degree of perfection.[19]

Also in the *Guide* itself, Thomsen emphasizes the importance of the find circumstances being carefully observed in archaeological investigations: 'As the artefacts, through the course of time, are always found covered and half hidden by dust, one should observe the greatest care, so as to be able to note the mutual relation between the deposited artefacts, which it is often more important to know than the artefacts themselves.'[20] This recommendation is moreover to be found in exactly the same wording in Thomsen's pamphlet *Scandinavian Artefacts and Their Preservation*, which had been published in 1832. In this pamphlet, which is primarily a guide to the methods of archaeological excavation and follow-up investigation, Thomsen also re-emphasizes the demand for greater accuracy in field investigations, as regards the find observations in particular.[21]

These views emerge even more strongly in an article published in 1832. Here, Thomsen puts forward views which reveal the critical attitude of the sober empiricist to the source material, and show that, on the relevant questions, he was far in advance of his time. He points out that the proper development of archaeological science does not only require a large material of antiquities in the museums: this material must also contain 'many specimens of the same thing, from which conclusions may be drawn with greater certainty'. However, the fact that the information about the find circumstances is often so poor reduces the source value of this material: 'Only too often, the exact circumstances of the find are forgotten, and later it is generally impossible to obtain reliable information about the associations in which the artefacts were found and other matters which might serve to yield information.' Clearly addressing himself to collectors of archaeological curiosities, Thomsen emphasizes 'that certainty about the correctness of the information is far more important for archaeological science than such very false tinsel'.[22]

Thomsen's understanding of the fundamental scientific importance of the find associations and his realization of the necessity of general surveys and consequently of public circulation of the material are also expressed in the joint Scandinavian find reports published in *Nordisk Tidsskrift for Oldkyndighed* (Scandinavian Journal of Archaeology) for 1832 and 1833.[23] The idea was to continuously present in this journal lists of new archaeological finds from all the Scandinavian countries. However, this far-sighted initiative was not continued and was only realized 130 years later.[24] In both volumes, Thomsen gave very detailed lists of Danish finds, with a – for that period – unusually strong emphasis on the find circumstances.[25] Here, we meet, for the first time, with a strictly topographical system of arrangement. It had not been chosen just for fun but, as Thomsen explained in a letter to Schröder, 'because it will not be without use for archaeological science to know where things are found together and what, on the other hand, never occurs in one place'.[26] The fact that the artefacts were not listed by categories but that each find was kept together as a unit is typical of Thomsen's way of regarding the artefacts not as isolated phenomena but as parts of a larger association.

In the above-mentioned letter, Thomsen stated as a reason for making the joint Scandinavian list of finds that he 'wished that we should first have some facts on which we might base hypotheses'. This statement illuminates, as with a flash of lightning, his long hesitation – cautious and sceptical as he was – to publish the Three-Age System, of the correctness of which he had long been convinced in his interior mind. The supply of closed finds and find observations had undoubtedly been poor from the very beginning of Thomsen's work. But, during the 20 years leading up to the publication of the

Guide, the collections at the Museum of Antiquities grew continuously under his direction, so that considerations of space compelled as early as 1832 a removal from the loft of Holy Trinity Church to larger premises in Christiansborg Castle.[27] But Thomsen was still hesitating at this time; the evidence must be further supplemented. Only 'when we have collected information for another couple of years will I take the liberty of presenting it and a couple of other observations which I believe will be conclusions'.[28]

As regards the significance of the find associations for the Three-Age System, Worsaae's testimony should also be taken into account. In *The Primeval Antiquities of Denmark* (1843), which Worsaae wrote at the age of 22 while he was still working under Thomsen at the Museum of Antiquities, he pointed out that the Three-Age System could scarcely have been constructed without observations of the find associations in particular: 'Thus, we would scarcely, in what has just been said, have been able to assign the artefacts to three consecutive ages if experience had not taught us that the artefacts

Fig. 13. Thomsen himself regularly demonstrated the collections of the Museum of National Antiquities in Copenhagen, here at Christiansborg Palace in 1846. Drawing by Magnus Pedersen.

which date from different ages are also generally found separately.'[29] This is precisely what Thomsen himself emphasizes in his autobiographical memoranda, in which he points out that, in re-arranging the artefacts in the Museum of Antiquities, he had paid especial attention to what had been found together and what had not been found together.[30] And what other than the evidence of the find associations in the form of assemblages can Thomsen have been referring to when, in order to convince Büsching, the Breslau (Wrocław) archaeologist, of the correctness of his system, he wrote to Büsching in 1823 and 1825, inviting him to visit the collections in Copenhagen and to acquaint himself with the many proofs of the Three-Age System which were to be found there?[31]

One detail which also shows that Thomsen was keenly alive to the importance of the find associations is that he realized that coins found together with artefacts were of particular interest in archaeological chronology. In the *Guide* he says that coins are 'especially noteworthy, because they can in general be dated and assigned to a certain period far more exactly and reliably than other artefacts. When they are found in association with other artefacts or are fixed to ornaments dating from prehistoric times, they become important in determining the ages of these artefacts'. He distinguishes four main groups of coins which are concerned in antiquity – Roman and Byzantine solidi, Roman denarii and Cufic silver coins.[32]

It has sometimes been asserted that in the *Guide* Thomsen displayed a kind of typological thinking.[33] The passage indicated runs as follows:

> For determining the approximate age of artefacts or, at least, to what period they relate, there is another guide which has hitherto been only little used with regard

Fig. 14. C. J. Thomsen. Drawing by V. Gertner.

to the Scandinavian artefacts – that of examining the forms and ornaments used, in order, by comparison and by noting which kinds are found in association, to find out the order in which changes accordingly take place and what one will be able, even from the ornaments, to assign to a certain period.

One is inclined to agree with Thomsen's own cautious reservations – that this was a line of research which had so far yielded little experience: 'Here also, our experiences are too few and too new, and we can only report the basic features of what we hope will later be more developed and definite.' In his examples, Thomsen confines himself in the main to assigning some characteristic Bronze Age ornaments to the Bronze Age (wave-band pattern, circle ornamentation, true spiral and double spiral) and some (late Iron Age) ornaments to the Iron Age (Style I and early Jellinge style). The only development analysis is expressed in the following words concerning the Bronze Age patterns: 'The first [i.e. the true spirals] seem to have originated from the ring ornaments and the double or composite [i.e. the double spirals] form the transition to the following styles [i.e. Style I and the early Jellinge style]'.[34]

As is clear, this developmental argument is in every respect unreasonable and unsuccessful. One may, of course, interpret it as an attempt at typological dating or grading, type analogy which had small chances of success, since as yet too little basic information about the material's chronological affiliation was obtainable. However, it must be stressed that, later in life, Thomsen never seems to have taken up any chronologically oriented, developmental analysis of archaeological material. It is also quite clear, as regards the Three-Age System itself – the division of prehistory into a stone age, a bronze age and an iron age – that there is no vestige whatever of any typological thinking, either in argumentation or in description.

Thus – to summarize a little here – there is no indication that, in formulating his Three-Age System, Thomsen started from any fundamental idea or any *a priori* conception about the cultural development, either in the *Guide* or in his other activities during the years concerned. It seems equally unreasonable to regard the Three-Age System solely as a practical way of arranging a large and confused museum material, an arrangement which, through Thomsen's intuition, happened to coincide with the evidence from the finds, which only afterwards confirmed the system. However many objects Thomsen had held in his hand, he would still never have been able to hit the mark in all the many chronological details, if he had not at the same time systematically observed 'what was found together and what not'.[35]

The decisive proof of the correctness of the Three-Age System was undoubtedly derived from observations concerning the find associations. Thomsen substantiated his basic scientific view in many different connections and campaigned for an increased general interest in the actual observation of finds. He realized quite clearly that the archaeological synthesis required a large source material. At the same time as he was, for his own part, endeavouring to get the widest possible overall view of the prehistoric source material in the entire Scandinavian cultural region, he recommended this as a general basis for all scientific archaeology. His own museum policy was governed by this conviction. As Worsaae later pointed out, Thomsen never hesitated to fight for his system and to demonstrate it.[36] The foundation of his steadfast conviction is to be found precisely in the empirical basis of the Three-Age System.

The fact that technological criteria are included in the definition of the Three-Age System does not by any means imply that the System came into being as a technological model. On the contrary, it is clear that Thomsen regarded his System primarily as a *chronological* division – a chronological aid in further investigations of cultural history. It is characteristic of Thomsen that in the *Guide* he nowhere makes any attempt to explain the changes in the course of cultural events which his division reflects. He only reports them.[37]

It is important to note the methodological background of the Three-Age System, because Thomsen's work became the fixed starting-point for all further chronological research. The dating work which was carried out by the following generations of scholars appears only as an increasingly fine-meshed network of interpolations and insertions within the certainly wide but fixed frameworks constituted by the Three-Age System. Even the complicated system of relative chronology used in modern archaeology has its permanent basis in Thomsen's work.

The Three-Age System may today appear to be commonplace and self-evident. In actual fact, it superseded a chronological view which, in spite of the attempts at system-building, was little better than total confusion. Thomsen's chronology avoided the usual fate of being refuted by new finds, precisely because it was based on a schematization of a large, collective number of find observations. Instead, the continual stream of new finds confirmed Thomsen's results and indirectly the empirical element in his working method. For this reason, the Three-Age System was accepted in Scandinavia rapidly and with no appreciable discussion. Part of its success was certainly due to the fact that

Fig. 15. Sven Nilsson (1787–1883), Swedish zoologist and prehistorian.

the System was not formulated as if the changes between the different ages were abrupt; on the contrary, they were described as being gradual transitions[38] of the kind which are better known in reality and which are comprehensible chiefly in empirical research.

In the preceding chapter, attention was drawn to the fundamental importance of the national collections formed at an early date in the Scandinavian countries for the rapid, scientific development of archaeology in these countries. I have earlier pointed out precisely this fact as an important precondition for the creation of the Three-Age System.[39] It was only through Thomsen's work at Copenhagen that the great collections there were organized in such a way as to enable a satisfactory survey to be made. Thanks to that, the Copenhagen collections were the first in Europe to be both representative of a large, cultural region and sufficiently well arranged to make an effective, scientific analysis possible.

Thus, it was not by chance that Thomsen in particular should be the man to codify the Three-Age System and to become its actual originator. Thomsen was undoubtedly the first person to acquire, by seeing for himself, a good survey of a comparatively large, source material, consisting of collective finds from a large, coherent, cultural area. He thereby became the first to be able to demonstrate in a convincing manner the hypothesis, which had earlier been suggested by many antiquarians without gaining a hearing, because it was grounded more intuitively and speculatively than empirically.

NOTES

1 Vedel Simonsen 1813, p. 76, note 1.
2 Petersen 1938, pp. 22ff.; cf. B. Hildebrand 1937–8, pp. 309ff.
3 Daniel 1943, pp. 13ff., 1950, pp. 43ff., 1967, pp. 90ff.; Rodden 1981; Montelius 1905, pp. 185ff.; Weibull 1923, pp. 247ff.; B. Hildebrand 1937–8, pp. 116–32 and 310–3 (cf. pp. 732–6); Rydbeck 1943b, pp. 170ff.
4 Danneil 1836; Lisch 1837.
5 Seger 1930, pp. 3ff.; Eggers 1959, pp. 43ff.; cf. H. Hildebrand 1886, pp. 357ff., 1887, pp. 128ff.; Hermansen 1934, pp. 100–6; Petersen 1938, p. 56; B. Hildebrand 1937–8, pp. 735f.
6 B. Hildebrand 1937–8, pp. 330–60 and 573–84; Hermansen 1934; Eggers 1959, pp. 32–52; cf. H. Hildebrand 1887, pp. 128ff.; Thomsen 1858.
7 B. Hildebrand 1937–8, pp. 573–84, 611ff., 677ff. and 711.
8 Andersen 1960, pp. 121–7.
9 Thomsen 1836, pp. 27–90.
10 Thomsen 1836, pp. 59ff.
11 Daniel 1943, pp. 5ff., 1950, pp. 43ff. and 50f., 1967, pp. 92ff. and 111; Piggott 1960, pp. 89f.; Heizer 1962, pp. 259ff.; Clarke 1968, pp. 10f.
12 Thomsen 1836, pp. 58ff.
13 Thomsen 1836, pp. 40, 58 and 60.
14 Thomsen 1836, pp. 32, 48, 53, 57ff.
15 Thomsen 1836, p. 59.
16 Seger 1930, pp. 4 and 6.
17 Thomsen 1836, pp. 32 and 58.
18 B. Hildebrand 1937–8, pp. 352ff.
19 Letters from Thomsen to J. H. Schröder dated 2 June 1821 and Febr. 1822; (Uppsala University Library G 263 1). My italics.
20 Thomsen 1836, p. 88.

21 Thomsen 1831, p. 2; the introductory pages of this pamphlet are reproduced almost verbatim on pp. 87–90 of the *Guide*.
22 Thomsen 1832a, pp. 420f.
23 *Nordisk Tidsskrift for Oldkyndighed*, 1, 1832, pp. 173–420, 2, 1833, pp. 169–92 and 247–351.
24 *Flit i Fält* (1967).
25 Thomsen 1832c, 1833.
26 Letter from Thomsen to J. H. Schröder dated 14 March 1832. (Uppsala University Library G 263 1).
27 Mackeprang 1939, pp. 6ff.
28 See note 25.
29 Worsaae 1843, p. 60. English translation 1849a.
30 Thomsen 1864.
31 Seger 1930, p. 6.
32 Thomsen 1836, pp. 81ff.
33 B. Hildebrand 1937–8, pp. 728, 1943, p. 104; Furumark 1950, pp. 5f.
34 Thomsen 1836, pp. 61ff.
35 Thomsen 1864.
36 Worsaae 1866a, p. 114.
37 Padberg's allusion to Cuvier's catastrophe theory as the background to the Three-Age System is not convincing (Padberg 1953, p. 21, note 8). It then seems more reasonable to test this idea as regards the marked partiality shown by Worsaae, Sven Nilsson and their contemporaries for popular immigrations as the explanation of the great changes in the artefact material, for example, at the beginning of the Bronze and Iron Ages (Worsaae 1843, pp. 21f., 37f. and 102ff.; Nilsson 1838–43, Chapter 6 (1843), pp. 1ff. and 16ff.).

   Nilsson's view of evolution was rather that of romantic natural philosophy. He first discussed Lyell's theory of the gradual evolutionary series in his *Scandinavian Fauna* (1855) (Danielsson 1965, pp. 167ff.).
38 Thomsen 1836, pp. 57ff.
39 Gräslund 1974, p. 95, 1981.

5

The works of Magnus Bruzelius

Before leaving the subject of the Three-Age System, I shall devote a few lines to the Swedish archaeologist Magnus Bruzelius, of Lund. Bruzelius was born in 1786 and was originally a physicist and chemist; he became *docent* at Lund University in 1809. Ten years later, he took holy orders and, from 1824 onwards, devoted himself entirely to his clerical duties. However, before that date, he took an intense interest in archaeology for a few short years and published a series of important archaeological works during the period 1816–23, i.e. precisely the years when Thomsen's Three-Age System was taking shape.

Lund in Sweden and Copenhagen in Denmark were almost neighbouring towns. Thomsen visited Bruzelius in Lund probably in 1820 and certainly in 1822. It is known that Thomsen read Bruzelius' archaeological works and that the two men corresponded with each other.[1] There are many indications[2] that, in his pioneering classification of stone artefacts entitled *Brief Survey of Scandinavian Stone Artefacts Dating from Heathen Times* (1832),[3] Thomsen was influenced by the classification of such artefacts made by Bruzelius in his *Specimen Antiquitatum Borealium* (1816–18).[4] The interesting thing is that, in several of his works, Bruzelius also suggested a chronological stratification into two or three eras.[5] The question is whether Bruzelius may have influenced Thomsen with regard to the Three-Age System.

If, in his early works, Bruzelius does not mention the Iron Age, this should not necessarily be interpreted as meaning that he did not reckon with the existence of such an age. Finds dating from the Iron Age were at this period still rather rare in Scania, and, in his early works, Bruzelius deals exclusively with archaeological materials dating from the Stone and the Bronze Ages. To begin with, he was rather vague in his datings. In his *Specimen Antiquitatum Borealium*, it is true, he describes clearly a stone-age period, but he does not assign any term to it.[6] In his first works, he does not draw any sharp distinction between the stone and the bronze periods in a chronological respect.[7] However, he draws such a distinction clearly and plainly in his book *Scandinavian Antiquities in Scania* (1822).[8]

Thus, it is not out of the question that Thomsen and Bruzelius may have mutually influenced each other as regards the overall chronological view of prehistory. On the other hand, Bruzelius' experience was restricted to Scania and, in any case, he did not expound in writing any detailed argumentation about chronological stratification in archaeology. However, it seems to be reasonable to include Thomsen's personal acquaintance with Bruzelius and his knowledge of Bruzelius' scientific work as an important part of the large background material on which Thomsen based his chrono-logical synthesis.

Bruzelius' works were strangely disregarded by the following generations of Swedish archaeologists. However, they are worth rescuing from oblivion. Bruzelius did not mechanically repeat the vague indications of periodic divisions of prehistory which had previously been given by Lund scholars such as Retzius and Sjöborg.[9] Bruzelius was actually the first Scandinavian archaeologist to describe in writing a division of prehis-tory based on factual find observations. But he was, above all, an independent and empirically oriented scholar.

As an example, I may mention Bruzelius' account of 1822 in the excavation of a passage grave in the parish of Kvistofta in Scania – one of the most remarkable works in early Swedish archaeology.[10] The finds were numerous and consisted exclusively of objects made of stone and amber, together with human and animal bones. It may have been Bruzelius' experience of this excavation which finally made him realize that the period of the stone artefacts would have to be distinguished as the first, independent period. He writes: 'If there were in history an epoch which could be designated "the stone age" . . . one would unhesitatingly assign the Åsa mound to this most remote age. In the absence of metals, flint was in this country the most suitable material both for weapons and for tools.' And he continues: 'No trace of metal could be found in the whole mound, in spite of the most careful examination.' He thereby emphasizes clearly that it was observations of the find associations which justified his distinguishing the stone age from the metal age. Bruzelius put forward similar arguments in a lecture entitled *The Dates and Uses of the Scandinavian Stone Artefacts*, which he gave in December 1822 and printed the following year. In this lecture, he points out, as a general archaeological observation, 'that stone instruments are fairly seldom found together with metal instruments'.[11] These examples, dating from 1822, are probably the earliest in Scandinavian archaeological literature of how observations of the concrete find circumstances were made the basis of chronological conclusions of universal validity.

We find here in Bruzelius' work the same, basic, empirical principle which was so consistent a feature of Thomsen's archaeological work. Bruzelius' archaeological writings bear witness throughout to the sober approach of a matter-of-fact empiricist. It is symptomatic that Bruzelius, just like Thomsen, emphasizes that it is important that the archaeological material should be reported and described properly, in order to enable conclusions of some scope to be drawn. He complains about the farmers' reckless treatment of the ancient remains and, like Thomsen and later Bror Emil and Hans Hildebrand, he pleads for the creation of national museums of archaeology.[12] Bruzelius' own works are on an – for their time – unusually high level, as regards both the field observations and the manner of reporting them. Reverting to the above-mentioned, passage-grave excavation, it will be observed that Bruzelius did not, as was usual at that time, only note that the finds came from the grave; he reports instead the positions of the different finds in relation to each other. In actual fact, he carried out the excavation on a horizontal-digging principle, many generations before such a procedure again became topical in Sweden. It was equally uncommon that he excavated not only in the burial chamber of the passage grave but also in the entrance passage and indeed even a little outside the passage, a procedure which we do not meet with later until well into the present century. The picture of Bruzelius' scientific foresight also includes his inter-disciplinary approach, which was here manifested in the facts that he was able to add to the archaeological description an analysis of the human bones, made by an anatomist, and an analysis of the animal bones, made by a zoologist (no less a person than Sven Nilsson, who was later also well known in archaeological circles).[13]

NOTES

1 B. Hildebrand 1937–8, pp. 315ff., 326ff. and 335.
2 Weibull 1923, pp. 251f.; B. Hildebrand 1937–8, pp. 315ff. and 331f.
3 Thomsen 1832b.
4 M. Bruzelius 1816–18.
5 M. Bruzelius 1816, p. 54, 1816–18, Part 1, pp. 3f., 1820, p. 100, 1822, pp. 304ff. and 1823, pp. 53ff.
6 M. Bruzelius 1816–18, Part 1, pp. 3f.
7 For example, M. Bruzelius 1820, p. 100.
8 M. Bruzelius 1822, p. 304.
9 B. Hildebrand 1937–8, pp. 301ff.
10 M. Bruzelius 1822.
11 M. Bruzelius 1823, pp. 53f.
12 M. Bruzelius 1816–18, Part 3, p. 21, 1817, p. 190, and 1820, p. 89.
13 M. Bruzelius 1822, pp. 291ff., 298ff. and 328ff.

6

The Stone Age:
the division into two and three periods

The kitchen middens

The further developments in Nordic archaeological research in the mid nineteenth century bear to an extraordinary large extent the stamp of Jens Jacob Worsaae. Most of the essential advances in research achieved during this period are associated with his name. Unlike anyone before him, Worsaae carried on excavation activities of epoch-making significance. He also had an extraordinary command of the archaeological material, not only in his home-country but in a wider international context, and he was the first to place the prehistoric monuments in a wider comparative context. He has rightly been called the founder of comparative archaeology. Worsaae also had a remarkable ability to interpret the historical information of the archaeological source material. However, he did not show any marked aptitude for or interest in detailed analysis of archaeological artefacts and types. Worsaae was first and foremost oriented towards historical and social perspectives, but his ability to grasp the universal and his knowledge of the material also gave him an eye for chronological essentials. His name is closely associated with the most important chronological advances made in the mid nineteenth century – the division of the Stone Age and the Bronze Age into two periods each and the Iron Age into three.

The investigation of the Stone Age occupies a comparatively obscure place in the history of nineteenth-century archaeology. The development of methods of relative chronology was devised mainly within the framework of the two metal ages. It was only at a fairly late stage (mainly during the last 60 years) that the relative chronology of the Nordic Stone Age acquired a fixed form, and then moreover it did so chiefly with the support of various, other, scientific disciplines. One important, contributory reason for this state of affairs was undoubtedly the *extraordinary* paucity of collected finds with a limited, chronological range dating from the Stone Age, considered as a whole. Single-grave finds of the type which essentially supports the relative chronology of the metal ages are available in large numbers mainly only from the Battle-Axe Cultures of Jutland and Sweden. Accordingly, only for them in particular has it been possible to draw up such detailed schemes of relative chronology as are common as regards the Bronze and Iron Ages.

The Danish kitchen middens provided the key to the first chronological division of the Nordic Stone Age. Japetus Steenstrup, the zoologist, had been concentrating his attention on the shell banks of northern Denmark ever since 1827. On the basis of the artefacts and other remains of human activity which he found there, he dated their origin to a period *after* the original settlement of Denmark. But he gave a geological explanation of the actual existence of these heaps of mussel shells – they had naturally been washed up out of the sea.[1]

Together with Steenstrup and the geologist Forchhammer, Worsaae in 1848 was included in an interdisciplinary commission to carry out a geological and archaeological investigation of the Leire district, with a view to trying to elucidate certain problems concerning the elevation of the land and the sea-level. The finds in the shell banks naturally came into the picture in this connection[2] and the commission was later given a wider remit. The discovery in 1850 of the enormous shell bank at Meilgaard on Djursland, with its abundant finds of implements and bone remains, was of decisive importance. As Worsaae points out in a diary entry in September 1850, these enormous piles of oyster shells must represent the remains of meals eaten by Stone Age people.[3] This was the beginning of several years of interdisciplinary study by Worsaae, Steenstrup and Forchhammer, the results of which unequivocally confirmed Worsaae's first impressions.[4] The work was continued and extended in the next few years and investigations were carried out on a number of shell banks.[5] By the end of the 1850s, over 50 shell-bank dwelling sites had been recorded, chiefly in northern Jutland and northern Zealand[6] but also in Scania.[7]

However, Worsaae gradually observed that these finds were of a quite different character from the Stone Age finds previously known. He gave his first indication of a division of the Stone Age in the autumn of 1857 in public lectures at the University of Copenhagen. He presented his observations in more detail in March 1859 in a lecture to the Royal Danish Academy of Sciences and Letters, in whose *Oversigt* it was published in the following year as the first part of the classic paper entitled *A New Division of the Stone and Bronze Ages*.[8]

Fig. 16. Jens Jacob Asmussen Worsaae (1821–85), Danish archaeologist, in his younger days.

Worsaae pointed out that 'the surprising thing about these finds is the homogeneity of their constituents'. The artefacts, in the form of 'rough-hewn flint axes, chisels, arrows, flint cores, nodules and flint flakes, axes made of deer antlers and a great many bodkins and implements made of bone', as well as the animal-bone material, were of a quite special kind. 'Most of the flint artefacts are completely rough and yet, judging by their large numbers, they were evidently used as they are.' But other finds, too, unconnected with either the shell banks or the stone-chamber tombs, tally with these finds, for example, those at Korsør Nor. 'Judging from all previous experience, one practically never discovers, in large, collected finds of stone artefacts, the roughest and the finest artefacts intermingled. They evidently constitute two very distinct groups.' The circumstances were the same whether the shell-bank dwelling sites were located on Limfjorden, on Zealand or in Scania.

> It is quite exceptional to find sharp-edged and finely polished, stone artefacts in the actual heaps of oyster shells. It is also very rare to find stone hammers and other, more sophisticated, stone artefacts in these heaps. In particular, neither the trimly shaped hammers, which are usually assigned to the beginning of the Bronze Age, nor the flint daggers with carved ornamentation on the hilts, which mark the culmination of flint manufacture, are hitherto known to have been discovered in these heaps of oyster shells . . . On the contrary, however, the stone-chamber tombs and the passage graves consistently yield smoothly shaped, finished and sharp-edged, flint artefacts and, in addition, neat stone hammers, amber ornaments and earthenware pots, several of which have quite tasteful shapes and decorations. It is completely unknown to me whether there have ever been discovered in a stone-chamber tomb or a passage grave in what is now Denmark such peculiar, rough, flint wedges as those which occur in such large, indeed in overwhelming numbers in the heaps of oyster shells.

On the basis of these observations, Worsaae considered that he could divide the Stone Age into two main periods: '(1) *The early Stone Age*, comprising the heaps of oyster shells and several of our coastal finds with their rough implements of flint and bone, and (2) *the late Stone Age*, comprising the large stone monuments, stone-chamber tombs and passage graves, with their neat artefacts of stone, bone, amber and burnt clay.'

As these quotations show, Worsaae very clearly demonstrated his arguments in favour of the division of the Stone Age into two periods. *The find circumstances* provided the chronological starting-point, to be precise, the *clearly differentiated, find* complexes of the shell-bank dwelling sites and in the stone-chamber tombs. His conclusions, which were moreover deduced from the study of a large material, were based on observations of *artefacts which were usually found together and artefacts which were not usually found together*. The operation also called for the distinguishing of types, i.e. the kinds of archaeological finds or other phenomena which recur (Worsaae himself does not use the term 'type', which did not generally come into use in Nordic archaeology until about 1870). However, the necessary comparison of similarities was of a very simple kind, owing to the fact that the two main groups of material differed so markedly from each other. As is often the case in the formation of archaeological types, the classification underlying Worsaae's division of the Stone Age into two periods was not the fruit of an independent method of classification by analogy; it is quite obvious that the two radically different, find complexes as such, were the starting-point for the observation of the type differences in the material. As Worsaae interpreted them, the finds from the shell-bank dwelling sites on the coasts and the stone-chamber tombs in the interior belonged to two distinct and unambiguous groups with few points of mutual contact.

It is precisely this fact which ultimately explains the diametrically opposed interpretations of the shell-bank finds which Worsaae and Steenstrup advocated and which were manifested in the subsequent, violent controversy between them.[9] Steenstrup firmly adhered to the earlier view, that the shell-bank finds and the finds in the stone-chamber tombs were contemporary and that they represented only 'two aspects of one and the same state of civilization'. Thus, the simpler and more primitive implements from the coastal dwelling sites would have belonged to the same people as sustained the stone-chamber-tomb culture, except that they were adapted to the simpler, practical needs of fishing and trapping. In a way, the dispute about the chronological division of the Stone Age was ultimately carried on at the level of historical interpretation. A contributory reason for the geologist Steenstrup's misinterpretation was certainly – as Worsaae also pointed out – his defective knowledge of the Stone Age finds outside the kitchen middens.[10]

As to the question of the *chronological order* of the two main groups of finds, i.e. which of them was the earlier and which the later, Worsaae evidently started from his view of the degree of primitiveness and the level of development of the material. The coastal finds were 'in short, artefacts which show no trace of metal or preparation with it but all of which, both in their form and in the frequent use of the lighter material deer antler

Fig. 17. Japetus Steenstrup (1813–97), Danish zoologist. Drawing.

and bone, instead of stone, indicate the greater age'.[11] Moreover, the total absence in the shell banks of remains of other domestic animals than the dog was noted as a difference with regard to the cultural development.[12] Thus, the chronological method underlying the division of the Stone Age into two periods could best be likened to a simple, *contrasting, combination method*, in which the chronological order was then justified on the basis of cultural evolution.

Palaeolithic, Mesolithic and Neolithic

The finds in English and French caves of cultural remains in stratigraphic association with long-extinct species of animals were an important discovery which supported Worsaae's views.[13] These finds were highly topical just in the years around 1860.[14] Moreover, Worsaae had become personally acquainted with Boucher de Perthes' finds and researches on the spot in Abbeville as early as 1847, in connection with his long visit to England.[15] It is possible that the discovery of these finds, for which Lubbock, a few years later, coined the term 'Palaeolithic', helped to open Worsaae's eyes to the possibility that the kitchen middens might represent a separate, early, cultural phase in Denmark. In a lecture in January 1861 and in his published controversy with Steenstrup, Worsaae moreover drew up a development scheme for the Stone Age with the western-European cave finds as the earliest, followed by the kitchen middens, and with the stone-chamber tombs and their environment representing the latest stage.[16] This was probably, as far as I know, the first time in the history of archaeology that a process of development was outlined for the Stone Age, including *all* the three periods which were later to be regularized under the designations of Palaeolithic, Mesolithic and Neolithic.

The terms 'Palaeolithic' and 'Neolithic' were coined in 1865 by the English archaeologist Sir John Lubbock in his book *Prehistoric Times*.[17] It may be mentioned that in this book Lubbock did not accept Worsaae's interpretation of the Danish middens as belonging to a separate period in the early Stone Age but regarded them as belonging to an early phase of the late Stone Age.[18] As regards the term 'Mesolithic' it was not coined by Otto Torell, the Swedish geologist, as has been stated.[19] Torell used the term in a paper written for the archaeological congress in Stockholm in 1874 and published two years later.[20] The Irish archaeologist Hodder Westropp seems to have used the term as early as 1866 in a lecture.[21] Westropp used the term 'Mesolithic' also in his book *Pre-historic phases* (1872).[22] Binford's statement,[23] that A. C. Carlyle, an English archaeologist who worked in India between 1868 and 1888, coined the term 'Mesolithic', is hardly correct either. It is apparently traceable back to a misinterpretation of the words of John Allen Brown, who wrote on the occasion of an exhibition of Carlyle's Stone Age finds in London in 1888 'to which he [scilicet Carlyle] *applied* the term Mesolithic'.[24]

The terms 'Mesolithic' and 'Neolithic' were for a long time sparingly used in the Nordic countries. The term 'Neolithic', for instance, came into general use only after the Second World War, primarily under the influence of C. J. Becker's book *Mosefundne Lerkar* (1948).[25]

NOTES

1 Steenstrup 1848, pp. 7–11.
2 Forchhammer and Steenstrup 1848, pp. 62–72.
3 Petersen 1938, pp. 181–5 (cf. pp. 197–9). Petersen here also discusses the problem of the right of scientific priority to this observation (1938, pp. 166–203). Cf. Worsaae 1852a, pp. 98ff.
4 Steenstrup 1851a, pp. 1–31, and 1951b, pp. 179–222.
5 Steenstrup 1853, pp. 14–24, 1854, pp. 191–7 and 204–7, 1855a, pp. 1–20 and 52, and 1855b, pp. 131f.
6 Worsaae 1860a, p. 7.
7 N. G. Bruzelius 1854a, pp. 197–204.
8 Worsaae 1860a, pp. 5–13.
9 Steenstrup 1860, Worsaae 1862a, Steenstrup 1862a and 1862b, Worsaae 1862b.
10 Worsaae 1862b, p. 20.
11 Worsaae 1860a, p. 7.
12 Worsaae 1862a, pp. 55ff.
13 Worsaae 1860a, pp. 10f., 1860b, pp. 33ff. and 1862a, pp. 59ff.
14 Daniel 1967, pp. 57–89 and 1975, pp. 57–67.
15 Bibby 1957
16 Worsaae 1862a, pp. 62ff. Cf. Daniel 1975, pp. 87ff.
17 Lubbock 1865, pp. 2f.
18 Lubbock 1865, pp. 194ff., and 1872, pp. 246ff.
19 Obermaier 1927, p. 154, Niklasson 1955, pp. 46ff.
20 Torell 1876, p. 876.
21 Daniel 1967, p. 260.
22 Westropp 1872, p. 65, cf. the theme on p. xxiv.
23 Binford 1972, pp. 421f.
24 Brown 1889, p. 139 (my italics).
25 Becker 1948, p. 9; cf. Brøgger 1925.

7

The Bronze Age: the division into two periods

During the nineteenth century, settlement sites dating from the Bronze Age were practically unknown in Scandinavia. On the other hand, there was at an early date a good supply of closed finds, primarily grave finds dating from both the early and the late Bronze Age. The state of affairs was quite different as regards the Stone Age and at least parts of the Iron Age. This situation came to characterize to a large extent the investigation of these three ages, especially as regards chronology. Therefore, it seems natural that the Bronze Age was the first of these three periods for which it was possible to draw up a detailed, internal chronology.

The first to clearly claim that the Bronze Age could be divided into an early and a late period was the Swedish archaeologist Nils Gustaf Bruzelius. He expressed his views in a paper entitled *An Account of Several Archaeological Sites in Scania and Southern Halland Excavated in 1853 and 1854* published in a Danish journal. Bruzelius based his results on excavations and observations made in the field. He noticed that, when both cremation graves and inhumation graves were found in the same Bronze Age barrow, the cremation graves were consistently encountered higher than, and occasionally on top of, the inhumation graves. He concluded from this that 'a new mode of burial came into use' in the course of the Bronze Age.[1]

The interesting thing is that Bruzelius claims that his conclusions are universally valid: 'If one were to venture to draw any conclusions from the above, they would be as follows: (1) that in large barrows, in which several corpses, both uncremated and cremated, have been interred, the former are always at the bottom and are consequently the oldest.'[2] Bruzelius repeated these views in the second edition of *Swedish Antiquities*,[3] published as a thesis in 1860, after he had found them further confirmed by continued field observations.[4] In this connection, we may disregard the fact that Bruzelius simultaneously arrived at the wrong conclusion, that 'women were almost always cremated'.[5] He was no doubt misled by the fact that most of the then known Bronze Age graves with uncremated corpses contained male objects.

At this time, numerous finds had come to light from Bronze Age barrows in Denmark, some as a result of careful excavations and supplementary investigations. The observations and experiences of these finds had similarly convinced Worsaae that the Bronze Age could be divided into two periods precisely on the basis of the burial customs. He presented his views in the above-mentioned paper of 1860, *A New Division of the Stone and Bronze Ages*, which became the classic reference and the starting-point for subsequent research into the relative chronology of the Bronze Age.[6] The prerequisite condition was again the well-known fact that Bronze Age barrows so often contain several burials. That the practice of cremation was mainly associated with the end of the Bronze Age was, according to Worsaae, demonstrated 'chiefly by the circumstance that, so far as is known, cremated corpses, together with bronze artefacts, have never been found at the bottom of a burial mound and above them uncremated corpses dating from the same age, whereas we have considerable experience, both from the northern countries and elsewhere, of finds of uncremated corpses at the bottom and cremated corpses above them in the same Bronze Age burial mounds'. Worsaae mentions as examples, *inter alia*, the barrows excavated at Jaegerspriis and at Jaegersborgs Dyrehave on Zealand: 'In all these mounds, the largest and heaviest stone cists were found at the bottom of the graves, but the smaller and lighter cists, which were evidently from a later period, were lying higher up. Finally, at the edges of all the mounds were found earthenware vessels or small stone cists containing burnt bones and ashes, in contrast to the earlier burials of uncremated corpses at the bottom of the mounds'.

Full-length and smaller stone cists containing burnt bones had also been discovered. Such a cist with burnt bones might also be the main burial at the bottom of a barrow, but 'round the edges lie the smaller graves, consisting of cinerary urns filled with burnt bones and ashes and surrounded with small cobbles'. Worsaae is inclined to attribute the oak-coffin graves found in southern Jutland, which 'must chiefly have held uncremated corpses', to a late stage of the early Bronze Age on account of the recurrent observation of their association with burnt bones.

It may also be noted that the Danish archaeologist Vilhelm Boye in 1858 briefly expressed views similar to those of Worsaae and Bruzelius, based on observations made during the excavation of a barrow containing many graves on the island of Møn: 'As the whole skeletons were lying at the bottom of the mound, they must have been placed

Fig. 18. Nils Gustaf Bruzelius (1826–96), Swedish archaeologist.

there first and are consequently to be assigned to an earlier part of the Bronze Age than the burnt bones, which lay above them. Finally, the stone cists seem to have been deposited at an even earlier date in the same period.'[7] It is not clear whether Boye considered the observation to be universally applicable to the Bronze Age. However, there is no doubt that his chronological division is based on stratigraphical observations that are just as refined as those of Bruzelius and Worsaae.

How much these scholars may have been dependent on each other is difficult to establish but is of little significance for the purpose of this study. Even apart from the fact that Boye may have had access both to Bruzelius' printed article and probably to Worsaae's views, which had been briefly presented in the autumn of 1857 in university lectures at the National Museum in Copenhagen,[8] his views can hardly be interpreted as an independent and well-thought-out conception of the burial customs of the Bronze Age. Even as late as the end of the 1860s, Boye expressed serious misgivings about precisely this idea of a division of the Bronze Age into two periods on the basis of the burial customs.[9]

Bruzelius' contribution to the division of the Bronze Age came to be overlooked. Not even Oscar Montelius, from whom practically all the further development of the Bronze Age chronology emanated, seems to have noticed Bruzelius' writings. Though he repeatedly mentioned the division of the Bronze Age into two periods as the starting-point for his chronological work, he only referred to Worsaae's work.[10] However, even if Worsaae was not the first to put forward the hypothesis about the division of the Bronze Age into two periods, his detailed presentation of the idea gave it its penetrating power and rapidly made it common scientific property.

As an additional confirmation of the correctness of their conclusions, both Worsaae and Bruzelius state that the German scholar Friedrich Lisch, in his investigations in

Fig. 19. Vilhelm Boye (1837–97), Danish archaeologist.

Mecklenburg, had come to a similar conclusion independently of them but on similar grounds, i.e. that inhumation was the oldest burial custom during the Bronze Age.[11] But, when a closer scrutiny is made of the references which they quote,[12] and also of other works published by Lisch at this time,[13] it is made quite clear that they read too much into Lisch's comments on his investigations. At this period Lisch had not yet freed himself from the common notion that cremation graves and inhumation graves were in general contemporaneous. His interpreting of the two burial customs as contemporaneous phenomena, representing only different sexes, peoples or families, show how far he still was from Worsaae's and Bruzelius' chronological view. It should be noted, however, that Lisch had no access to the distinct stratigraphy which had guided Bruzelius and Worsaae. It is plain that his conclusions were coloured by his scanty source material, in which inhumation and cremation graves were on several occasions found lying close to each other at the same level in the barrow.

This example illustrates how extraordinarily dependent the early students of relative chronology were on the material of which they had experience and, in general, what a decisive role observations of the find circumstances played during the period when the systems of relative chronology were being established.

Now Worsaae did not only bring about a division of the Bronze Age into an early period with inhumation graves and a late period with cremation graves. He also presented a fairly detailed schedule of the changes in the Bronze-Age burial customs and the design of the grave caches.[14] This schedule may be summarized as follows, in chronological order from the earliest to the latest:

(1) Large stone cists with thick stone lids.
(2) Full-length stone cists which had been covered with wooden planks.
(3) Uncremated corpses within a stone frame or covered with stones (in these cases, the corpse had probably originally lain in a wooden coffin).
(4) Oak coffins containing uncremated corpses and sometimes also burnt bones.
(5) Full-length stone cists with burnt bones wrapped in cloth.
(6) Smaller stone cists containing burnt bones.
(7) Earthenware vessels containing burnt bones, surrounded by pebbles.

The general picture of the development of the burial customs in the Bronze Age which Worsaae sketches here differs little from the view of the matter which prevails today. It has mainly been based on a procedure which closely combines the contrasting and chronologically orienting *stratigraphy* with the *grouping* and, to some extent, *grading combination method* (a combination stratigraphy).

A good description of the grouping and, in part, grading combination method in its simple form, which was the essence of the chronological method in archaeological research in the mid nineteenth century, was given by J. B. Sorterup in 1846 in a guide to the collections in the Archaeological Museum at Christiansborg. Sorterup begins by explicitly emphasizing the necessity of obtaining good information about the circumstances and he notes that 'antiquities which are found in graves can generally be assigned to one of these three periods from the above-mentioned dissimilarity of the graves themselves and from what they are found in association with . . . On the other hand, what is not found in graves but in unspecified circumstances can only be determined by its agreement with what has already been determined'.[15]

It is not possible to attain complete clarity about the deductive process which preceded Worsaae's drawing up of his grave-type schedule for the Bronze Age. However, through the examples which he quoted, Worsaae himself gives us information about the minimum of stratigraphic fact that he had to guide him. The whole schedule can be more easily illustrated by the numbers which he affixed to the above-mentioned grave types. The barrows at Jaegerspriis and Jaegersborgs Dyrehave yielded the stratigraphy 1–5–6/7 and those at Kjeldby on Møn the series 3–6–7.[16]

Furthermore, the series of pairs 1–2, 2–7, 3–7, 4–7, 5–7 and 6–7 occurred in different contexts. However, the mutual relation between the groups 2, 3, 4 and 5 cannot be directly deduced from these series. Nevertheless, it no doubt emerged that 2, 3 and 4 should be placed before 5 as an evident conclusion from Worsaae's extraordinarily abundantly documented observation that cremation graves were in general later than inhumation graves. Moreover, Worsaae justifies his placing of 4 immediately before 5 by saying that though the oak-coffin graves contained unburnt bones, they were also often associated with cremation graves. According to him, group 1 was directly linked with the Stone Age by finds of artefacts of Stone Age type, for example, flint daggers, and is also quite formally connected with Stone Age graves containing massive stone cists with stone lids. Group 2 could be placed early in the schedule through examples of direct superimposition on group-1 graves and through the fact that they were somewhat smaller in size and lacked stone lids, i.e. their 'arrangement and form differed' more from the 'cist-shaped chambers' of the Stone Age.[17]

It will accordingly be seen that the placement of group 5 and also of group 4 is a direct consequence of Worsaae's main observation concerning the chronological relation of the inhumation graves and the cremation graves. The placement of groups 1 and 2 before the rest was self-evident, owing to the fact that they were the only groups which had no connection with burnt bones.

By way of summary, it may be said that Worsaae's detailed classification of burial customs in the Bronze Age was obtained by *contrasting* and to some extent *grading combinations stratigraphy*, together with a small measure of free comparison of similarities.

The appearance of descriptive typology

Worsaae's schedule of the burial customs of the Bronze Age may be regarded as the first sign of a wider view of the possibilities of relative chronology. In actual fact, we here meet with an indication of typological reasoning or rather the *description* of a typological context, of a continuous process of transformation of cultural products. Worsaae's account heralds the typological mode of expression of a later generation:

> As the very oldest graves and as *an intermediate link* with those of the Stone Age
> . . . *The transitions* from the early to the late burial customs . . . *The more* the
> arrangement and the form of the graves of the stone cists *differ* from the cist-
> shaped chambers of the stone-chamber tombs and the passage graves, *the later*
> they must certainly be considered to be . . . It is, so to speak *a reminiscence* of the

earlier burial custom, when the corpses were buried uncremated, that the stone cists and the chambers should *still* be of considerable size, a man's full height. But this practice can hardly have *continued for long. Gradually*, as cremation became more widespread and established, the size of the stone cists also *became increasingly restricted*. The stone cist *now only needed to be large enough* to contain the burnt bones, either deposited loosely or collected in a cinerary urn, and in addition at most the dead man's weapons and jewellery.[18] (my italics)

Worsaae's account of the burial customs of the Bronze Age illustrates a stage in the development of methods of early archaeology which, in my opinion, had a great share in the genesis of the 'typological method' and the ideas associated with it. We have here an example of how the find contexts arouse the awareness of scholars of the close connection between forms, groups or types of slightly different dates and of the fact that features of the one can often be observed in the other. Worsaae undoubtedly did derive the basic knowledge that the burial customs of the Bronze Age had not changed abruptly, but step by step, just from the find contexts. They were the prerequisite of his description of the development of the grave types and provided the foundation for a chronological division which was so detailed that it became possible to observe a continuity in the changes.

However, *Worsaae's 'typology' is wholly descriptive*. It has not yet progressed from a passive, chronological description to an active, dating method. Such a step might seem to be a short one, but Worsaae did not use his observations to go a step further and develop an independent dating of grave types by a grading type analogy. He made no active investigations of 'typological' development. It may be that, in his heart of hearts, he had doubts about the validity of the details of his classification of grave types. This

Fig. 20. J. J. A. Worsaae, at a mature age. Drawing by A. A. Jerndorff.

is indicated by the brief summary of the problem which he gave at the end of his account, for there he excludes all but the main idea of the division of the Bronze Age into two periods:

> For the time being, we may certainly safely halt at the conclusion which so many excavations of graves, both in Scandinavia and elsewhere, warrant us in drawing, namely *that the graves which contained uncremated corpses and bronze artefacts are, as a rule, older than those which held cremated corpses and bronze artefacts.* This is already a considerable advance, which immediately informs us of a hitherto unknown and remarkable transition from the Stone Age to the Bronze Age and which will undoubtedly in course of time bring in its train many more important items of information, to the advantage of the national archaeology in general.[19]

It is striking that Worsaae, like Bruzelius and Boye, made no attempt in this connection to bring the Bronze Age artefacts into the chronological discussion. He was evidently not ready to draw the conclusions from his classification of burial customs to assign also the artefacts in the graves to an early and a late group. It is true that he considered that he could perceive artistic and stylistic differences between an early and a late group of Bronze Age artefacts but he nevertheless states that 'if we otherwise compare the bronze artefacts which are unearthed from the probably oldest graves with those which are constantly found in the late graves, we shall hardly be in a position to demonstrate any conspicuous difference. Indeed, the finds have not yet been sufficiently differentiated'.[20]

This example also illustrates the fact that the combination method always requires type definitions, the making of which significantly determines the results of the combination dating, and that a careful type characterization is a precondition for an accurate chronological classification. It was undoubtedly simpler to classify roughly the grave material into types than the artefact material, and Worsaae never undertook a detailed analysis of the artefact material, which explains his inability to create a more detailed, artefact chronology on the basis of his stratigraphical observations. The systematic analysis of archaeological artefacts still played a subordinate role in the work of Worsaae and the generation of scholars to which he belonged. The development of artefact analysis instead became perhaps the most important contribution made by the next generation of scholars to the methodology of relative chronology, which, in consequence, also resulted in a detailed, artefact chronology with the aid of the closed finds.

NOTES

1 N. G. Bruzelius 1855b, p. 356.
2 N. G. Bruzelius 1854b, p. 257.
3 N. G. Bruzelius 1860, pp. 17ff.
4 N. G. Bruzelius 1857, pp. 74ff.
5 N. G. Bruzelius 1854b, p. 257.
6 Worsaae 1860a, pp. 13–25.
7 Boye 1858, p. 212.
8 Worsaae 1860a, pp. 5 and 17.

9 Boye 1869, pp. 169ff., cf. however 1866, p. 221.
10 Montelius 1885a, pp. 3ff.
11 Worsaae 1860a, p. 18; N. G. Bruzelius 1860, p. 49.
12 Lisch 1857a, pp. 279–87; Bruzelius also refers to Lisch 1858, pp. 279–84.
13 Lisch 1857b, pp. 287f., and 1859, pp. 267–9.
14 Worsaae 1860a, pp. 18ff.
15 Sorterup 1846, pp. 61f. and 68.
16 Worsaae 1860a, pp. 18f.
17 Worsaae 1860a, pp. 1ff.; cf. Boye 1869, pp. 101, 109f. and 117f. N. G. Bruzelius had already demonstrated series 3–6 (Bruzelius 1854b, pp. 350ff.).
18 Worsaae 1860a, pp. 18ff. Italics mine.
19 Worsaae 1860a, p. 25.
20 Worsaae 1860a, pp. 24ff.

8

The Iron Age:
the division into two and three periods

The Roman Iron Age

For the relative chronology of the Iron Age there came into existence a means of dating which had not affected the earlier chronological divisions of the Stone and Bronze Ages: the dating by means of written sources. It proved to be possible to use comparisons with continental archaeological material which had been directly or indirectly dated by historical means for a chronological division within the Iron Age. In this connection coins naturally occupy a special position. As a consequence, relative dating within the Iron Age was, paradoxically enough, constructed principally on the basis of historical, absolute dates. On the whole, absolute and relative dating entered into an inseparable union in the chronological system of the Iron Age. In constructing the general chronological framework of the Iron Age, direct analogy between artefact types evidently played a subordinate role.

The first serious attempt to delimit the Iron Age in absolute terms was made by Thomsen in his *Guide* (1836). It was through historical sources known that 'iron was in general use in the south' at the time of Julius Caesar, and Thomsen assumed that the Scandinavian Iron Age could also be traced back to a corresponding period.[1] In the same way, Rudolf Keyser, the Norwegian historian, took the statement by Tacitus that the Germans knew how to use iron to justify his conclusion that the Iron Age must have been established in the Scandinavian countries during the second century A.D.[2]

However, it proved to be difficult to gain a hearing for such hypotheses among the new, more puristic generation of scholars whose chief representative was Worsaae and who sought primarily to establish facts on the basis of the purely archaeological material. Thus, it was decades before these early datings of the beginning of the Iron Age in northern Europe were generally accepted by Scandinavian archaeologists.

Before the middle of the nineteenth century most of the then known Iron Age finds were of Viking and late Iron Age dates, mainly from Norway and central Sweden. The fact that at that time Iron Age finds were far less common in Denmark and southern Sweden suggested to Worsaae the idea that the Iron Age there must have covered a shorter period of time and that, instead, the Bronze Age with its numerous finds lasted longer. As a result, in his early works, Worsaae dated the limit between the Bronze and Iron Ages in Denmark as late as the eighth and ninth century A.D.,[3] but some years later he moved it back to *c.* A.D. 700.[4] However, this did not mean that Worsaae did not realize that there were many finds which were either of Roman provenance or were strongly influenced by Roman culture. He even provided a comprehensive survey of these finds in 1849 in his article *Finds of Roman Antiquities in Denmark*.[5]

In those of his early numismatic works in which he dealt with finds of Roman coins in Scandinavia, Bror Emil Hildebrand did not present an absolute date for the onset of the Iron Age. He positively asserted, however, that the Roman silver denarii discovered in northern Europe could not have been deposited there later than the third century A.D. He maintained that coins, like other Roman products, must have reached the North via direct or indirect trade with Roman territories.[6] In contrast, Worsaae interpreted this exchange of goods as a very slow, indirect trade. Accordingly, the Roman products would not have reached northern Europe until long after the actual Roman era.[7]

The inhumation graves of the Roman Iron Age in Denmark, containing rich fittings, including imported Roman objects, were at that time usually contrasted with the large mounds of the late Iron Age, but in terms of social status rather than date. Thus, they were not chronologically distinguished from the late Iron Age graves.[8]

Notwithstanding that the number of finds of Roman provenance and showing Roman cultural influence had increased towards the middle of the century, Worsaae did not shift the limit for the onset of the Iron Age further back than 'the 5th or the 6th century A.D.'.[9] One restraining factor was certainly the fixation on Thomsen's definition of the Iron Age. Cutting weapons and implements of iron were still very rare among finds with Roman associations, as were, in fact grave finds. The discovery of the abundant finds in the bogs of western Denmark therefore had a liberating effect on the research situation.[10]

Almost every year from 1845 to 1852, objects discovered in connection with peat-cutting at Vimose near Allesø on the island of Fyn were sent to the Museum in Copenhagen. Particularly conspicuous were the many weapons and parts of weapons, which, on account of their excellent state of preservation, were at first interpreted, and even exhibited, as mediaeval. It was only when a new, large consignment arrived in 1853 that the contexts became clear. That the Vimose finds were prehistoric was shown by a scabbard-fitting of bronze[11] with runes of the same type as were already known from one of the Gallehus horns and a sheet-silver fibula from the Himlingeøie grave.[12] In 1853, as a result of this observation, Worsaae and Herbst jointly undertook a comparative analysis of the Vimose finds and the earlier finds in the museum which led to the acceptance of a native early Iron Age in Denmark.

The immediate significance of the Vimose finds lay in the fact that they comprised obviously native weapons and implements which could be co-ordinated with finds containing imported Roman objects, partly on account of the joint occurrence of both categories at Vimose and partly by analogies with Roman finds made in other places, especially the graves. In this way, the native iron culture could be convincingly linked for the first time with the Roman imports and the occurrence of an early Iron Age could be attested.

Let us consider Worsaae's first decisive observation (a). He had noticed that the Roman finds did not come to light in barrows but always in inhumation graves dug in natural sand and gravel banks. At that time, these graves had never yielded artefacts with the characteristic animal ornament. However, it was precisely such ornament that was found over and over again in the large barrows: 'Here, the weapons, the jewellery and the burial customs are of a completely different kind.' In the barrows, the dead were buried with their weapons, jewels, horses and riding gear, and these graves must therefore date from a different period. It was clear that this must be a later period than that of the 'common burial-places' from the discovery in the barrows of Byzantine coins, gold bracteates, Arabic coins etc., 'in brief, artefacts which point to a different and later origin'.[13]

The second main component in Worsaae's argumentation (b) consisted of a comparison between the Vimose finds and the related Roman and semi-Roman finds in the museum at Copenhagen.[14] This confirmed the 'connection and contemporaneity' of the two groups.[15] Herbst's account of his observations closely concurs with Worsaae's. He 'followed the given thread through a series of burial and bog finds' and thereby succeeded in 'clearly demonstrating a large measure of agreement between the edge fittings, various ornaments, etc. which occur in both types of finds'. It was 'thereby established that they belonged to the same period and that this period must, on account of the many Roman antiquities among the burial finds, have covered the first few centuries after the birth of Christ'.[16]

These conclusions were rapidly confirmed by new finds from bogs and graves, e.g. the Thorsbjerg, Nydam and Kragehul bog finds, all of which were, like Vimose, excavated by Conrad Engelhardt.[17] Thus, the dividing of the Iron Age into two periods was achieved in two ways: (a) by the method of *contrasting combination* (including the process of classification of types) and (b) by an independent comparison of similarities of form or decoration, a method of *horizoning analogy*. In addition, there is, of course, as a decisive chronological premiss for the argumentation, the generally accepted dating of the Roman imports to the time of the Roman emperors.

In his article entitled *The Varpelev Find* Herbst refers to the obvious fact that the result was achieved by observations of the find associations. His account takes in part

Fig. 21. Christian Frederik Herbst (1818–1911), Danish archaeologist.

the form of a general statement of method, which both illustrates the methodological consciousness of the Danish archaeologists of the middle of the nineteenth century, and explains their successful efforts to establish a basic chronological division of the past:

> However, the numerous collective, archaeological finds in the possession of the Museum are far more important for the study. It is these collective finds which obviously yield the greatest and most reliable profit for science, and therefore they have quite appropriately been called the documents and written sources of archaeological research. A collective find, that is to say, a find of antiquities which in the bowels of the earth is either surrounded by definite bounds, such as the walls of a burial chamber, or is lying in a place which is so limited as regards extent and depth in the soil that it is obvious that the antiquities were deposited at the same time and for the same purpose, thereby takes on a predominant importance for science. Sometimes a single such find, particularly when it is excavated under expert guidance and treated with care, can provide so much information about the purposes of the individual objects and about manners and customs at the time of its deposition . . . that it is of predominant importance even as an isolated find; but such finds are exceptional and in general finds first take on their true significance when compared with other, more or less homogeneous finds, whereby they come to form . . . a cable through which there runs a recognizable, guiding thread. Thus, it was by comparing finds that the most important of the discoveries that have emerged in the field of archaeological research in the last two decades was made, namely the demonstration of the existence of an early Iron Age.[18]

Here Herbst expresses his support of the markedly empirical research which characterized Danish archaeology in particular at that time. This research concentrated on find associations and was consequently interested in the quality of find observations, exhibiting a general aversion to speculation and loose analogies that had no immediate support in the find circumstances.

The middle Iron Age
The next phase in the construction of a chronological system for the Iron Age was distinguishing a separate stage between the already established Roman and late Iron stage. We again meet with the name of Worsaae. The proposal to delimit a middle Iron Age was first put forward in his book *The Antiquities of Schleswig and Southern Jutland* in 1865.

In this book Worsaae's main interest was not chronology, and his definition of the middle Iron Age was not very clear. Attention was concentrated, in the first place, on gold coins, especially the Byzantine solidi dating from the fifth and sixth centuries. In the second place, his attention was devoted to the native gold bracteates, which were regarded as imitations of Byzantine or eastern Roman Imperial coins and consequently as roughly contemporary with these coins, together with which they often appeared in closed finds. Large fibulae bearing animal ornamentation, some of which had been found together with gold bracteates, formed a second group of chronologically important native artefacts. The archaeological content of the period was mainly formulated

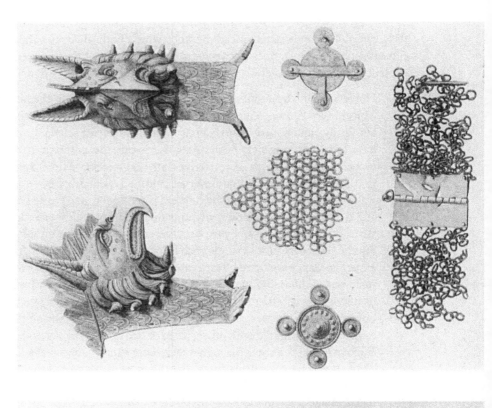

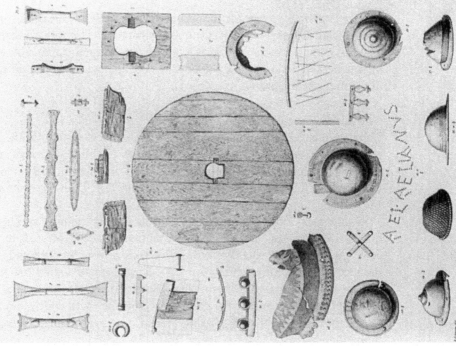

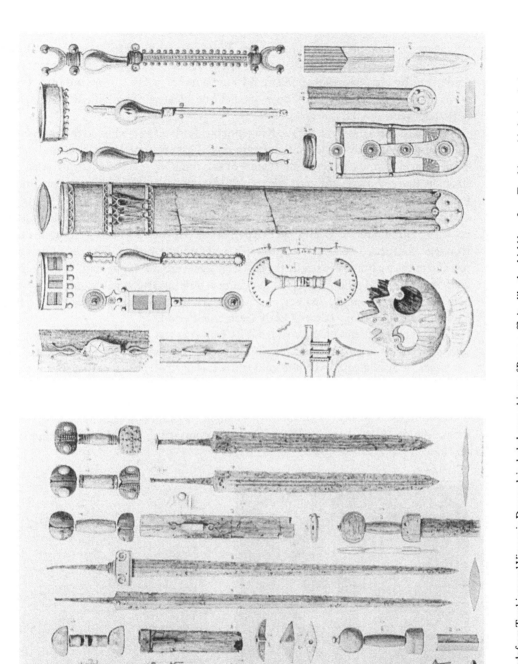

Figs. 22–23. The bog finds from Torsbjerg and Vimose in Denmark included some objects of Roman affinity, like the shield boss from Torsbjerg with the inscription *Aelius Aelianus* (opposite page, left), and the griffon heads from Vimose (opposite page, right). They helped, in the early 1850s, to assign the majority of the domestic objects in the bog finds (above) to the time of the Roman emperors, and thus to distinguish an early Iron Age. (After Engelhardt 1863 and 1869.)

only in terms of simple pictorial references. Worsaae's rapid sketch, however, indicated some of the archaeological elements most characteristic of this period and convinced his readers of the reasonableness of distinguishing a middle stage during the Iron Age. In terms of years, he delimited this stage, which he designated 'the middle Iron Age', to the period between *c.* A.D. 450 and 750.[19]

Engelhardt held the view that the Kragehul bog find was very close to this middle Iron Age in time or actually dated from its beginning. This prompted him, in his publication of the Kragehul find, 'to give a short view of this middle period'. He emphasized more strongly than Worsaae the part played by 'the many mutually concordant finds of Byzantine gold coins, gold bracteates and a distinctive type of fibula' (relief fibula). He also drew attention to the frequent use of the niello and cloisonné techniques and the practice of inhumation burial. Engelhardt's list of Danish finds dating from the middle Iron Age comprised 66 artefacts, primarily soil and bog finds.[20] The deliminations in relation to the early and especially the late Iron Age were still vague, but, with the solidi, gold bracteates and relief fibulas as the principal guiding artefacts, the middle Iron Age nevertheless stood out as a distinct, chronological horizon, corresponding broadly to the later concept of the Migration or Early Germanic Period.

Thus, the firm foundation for the middle Iron Age was the occurrence of the *historically dated* coins in closed finds containing native products. The gold bracteates were dated partly by analogies with the gold coins and partly by the fact that they occurred in finds together with gold coins. The relief fibulas were dated by being found with coins and bracteates. The relief fibulas could then be used as an independent dating element in closed finds. A *method of grouping combination* was applied, i.e. a horizoning combination dating in the horizon formation and a contrasting combination dating in the

Fig. 24. Conrad Engelhardt (1825–81), Danish archaeologist, at the age of 20. Oil-painting by E. J. Baumann.

delimination in relation to the early and late periods. There were also strong elements of historical dating. The further filling-in of the type and find contents of the period took place to a considerable extent by a grouping method, i.e. a *type-forming and type-contrasting analogy*.

NOTES

1 Thomsen 1836, p. 60.
2 Keyser 1839, pp. 448 and 450–62.
3 Worsaae 1841, pp. 158ff., and 1843, pp. 57ff. (1849a, p. 000).
4 Worsaae 1864a, p. 78, 1847, pp. 376ff., and 1852b, pp. 234d.
5 Worsaae 1849b, pp. 391ff.
6 B. E. Hildebrand 1844, p. 13; 1846, pp. vi f.
7 Worsaae 1843, pp. 53ff.; cf. 1858, p. 5, 1854, p. 58.
8 Worsaae 1843, pp. 81f.; cf. N. G. Bruzelius 1853, pp. 56ff.
9 Worsaae 1852b, p. 26.
10 Ørsnes has given an excellent summary of the course of events relating to the discovery of the early Iron Age, Ørsnes 1969, pp. xiii–xx.
11 Worsaae 1854, fig. 253, and Engelhardt 1869, Text-fig. 18.
12 Worsaae 1854, fig. 305b.
13 Worsaae 1858, pp. 6f.; cf. Worsaae 1860, p. 3.
14 Worsaae 1866b, p. 10; cf. Worsaae 1858, pp. 7ff., and 1860a, pp. 2f.
15 Worsaae 1858, p. 9.
16 Herbst 1865, pp. 4ff.
17 Engelhardt 1858, 1863 (Thorsbjerg), 1865 (Nydam), 1866, 1867a (Kragehul), 1858, 1867b, 1869 (Vimose).
18 Herbst 1865, pp. 2f.
19 Worsaae 1865, pp. 69ff.
20 Engelhardt 1867a, pp. 18ff.

9

The pre-Roman Iron Age

From the written sources, it had long been clear that, in technological terms, societies such as ancient Rome and pre-Roman Gaul belonged to the Iron Age. Guided by the information given by classical authors about the Germanic peoples, Thomsen early assumed that, in the Scandinavian countries, the Iron Age must have begun at some time around the birth of Christ.[1]

Of decisive importance for the evaluation of the early Iron Age in central and northern Europe were the overwhelmingly abundant finds which, over a succession of years from the middle of the century onwards, came to light at Hallstatt in the Salzkammergut in Austria and at La Tène near Neuchâtel in Switzerland. The Swede Nils Gustaf Bruzelius was one of the first European archaeologists to realize the significance of the burial finds at Hallstatt. In 1858 he made a thorough examination in Vienna and Linz of the still unpublished material from Hallstatt. From this, he concluded that the Iron Age in southern central Europe must have begun 'two centuries before the beginning of the Christian era'. Bruzelius was able to establish that the burial ground at Hallstatt reflected the transitional period between the Bronze Age and the Iron Age. The decisive fact was the absence of any trace of Roman imports or finds which showed the influence of Roman culture. It was not only that Roman coins were lacking (no coins whatever were found). Nor were any finds made which indicated that the art of writing had been known. On the other hand, Bruzelius was able to observe an influence from the sphere of 'Etrurian' culture. However, he did not use the Hallstatt finds in discussing the question of the dating of the beginning of the Iron Age in northern Europe.[2]

In his doctoral thesis, entitled *From the Iron Age*, published in 1869, Oscar Montelius discussed the dating of the earliest part of the Iron Age, *inter alia*, on the basis of the Hallstatt finds, which had then recently been published.[3] He seized upon precisely the same circumstances as Bruzelius had adduced. He added to them the observation that the bronze objects at Hallstatt had been made from the tin bronze which was common in the Bronze Age and not from the zinc-and-tin bronze which occurred more often in the Iron Age. He concurred with von Sacken's opinion,[4] that the burial field at Hallstatt dated from the second half of the first millennium B.C., possibly the fourth and third centuries.[5]

Montelius now introduced into the discussion the abundant, early Iron Age finds, especially weapons, from La Tène and Tiefenau in Switzerland, which had begun to come to light shortly after the middle of the century and which were first reported in scientific publications in 1858.[6] He agreed with the dating of these finds: the centuries immediately before the birth of Christ, a dating mainly based on the occurrence of Celtic coins, but when it came to dating the onset of the Scandinavian Iron Age, Montelius was very cautious, stating that the Iron Age began during the second century A.D. at the latest. However, he interpreted this only as a *terminus ad quem* and he thought it probable that iron appeared in the northern countries 'considerably earlier'. His hesitation was doubtlessly due to the prevailing lack of good chronological fix-points.[7]

The first archaeologist to use the Hallstaff and La Tène finds for chronological purposes with decisive effect was Hans Hildebrand. In *Towards a History of the Fibula*, he was, in the early 1870s, able to arrange these two complexes as two successive horizons at the end of the Bronze Age and the beginning of the Iron Age in central and northern Europe.[8] It was also Hildebrand who, at the archaeological congress in Stockholm in 1874, launched 'Hallstatt' and 'La Tène' as chronological and cultural concepts.[9] The final division of the European La Tène culture into the classical groups I–III was made a decade later by the German archaeologist Tischler.[10]

The early Iron Age on Bornholm

This was the situation when Emil Vedel, the prefect of the Danish island of Bornholm, carried out between 1868 and 1872 a large-scale and systematically arranged programme of field work on the early Iron Age on Bornholm – work which was to alter the picture of the earliest part of the Iron Age in northern Europe in a decisive and permanent fashion. With his assistants, Vedel made an inventory of no less than 4,000 graves from this period in 34 different burial grounds, and he excavated as many as 1,550 of these graves. He also rapidly published the results in two long articles entitled *The Cremation Patches on Bornholm* and *The Early-Iron-Age Burials on Bornholm*.[11]

Vedel's works were in several respects ahead of their time. They differed from earlier works not only on account of the extraordinary size of the field programme but also on account of his unusually penetrating analysis of cemeteries, which was not imitated until in the modern, sophisticated, chronological methods. As an amateur he was also little influenced by the obscure, written sources which had long fostered the idea that the early Iron Age culture in Scandinavia was associated with a mass migration. Vedel, instead, was able to show with detailed archaeological arguments that the source material bore unequivocal witness to a continuity of culture and population from the Bronze Age to the Iron Age and that this continuity must have applied to Denmark as a whole.[12] He even ventured, for the first time and exclusively on the basis of archaeological material, to push the dividing-line between the Bronze and Iron Ages well on the far side of the magic date of Christ's birth. This conclusion was based partly on a calculation of the population represented by the numbers of graves and partly on the observation that a large proportion of the finds were wholly uninfluenced by Roman taste. After first having dated the beginning of the Iron Age on Bornholm to *c.* 400/300 B.C., he finally decided in favour of the more cautious dating of *c.* 150/100 B.C.[13] To all appearances, he made this adjustment after having read the recently published, first volume of Hans Hildebrand's *Towards a History of the Fibula* in which Hildebrand argued that fibulae of the type included in Vedel's second cremation-patch group displayed a distinct 'Roman' influence.[14]

Vedel presented a division of the early Iron Age on Bornholm into six periods according to the types of grave, each with its characteristic artefact type. These groups are as follows:

Cairns
Cremation patches, 1st group
   ''   2nd ''
   ''   3rd ''
Inhumation graves
Cist tombs

The cairn group was assigned to the transitional period between the Bronze Age and the Iron Age. Vedel reckoned that almost two-thirds of the cremation patches belonged to the first group and, consequently, that this group represented the same proportion of the time when this form of burial prevailed. The inhumation graves were referred mainly to the transition to the middle Iron Age and the cist tombs were assigned to the middle Iron Age.[15]

Vedel's periods cannot be directly transferred to the period concept now in use. Generally speaking, the cairn group corresponds to the transitional period from the Bronze Age and the initial period of the Iron Age, the first group of the cremation patches to the late, pre-Roman Iron Age and the second group to the Early Iron Age.

Vedel had thereby introduced the concept of the pre-Roman Iron Age in northern Europe and he had convincingly established in a direct archaeological way the contact between the Bronze and the Iron Ages. His results were of great importance for research throughout the Scandinavian countries, although it was some time before they were recognized as being generally valid, primarily because of the lack of confirmatory material in other regions.

Fig. 25. Emil Vedel (1824–1909), Danish archaeologist. Drawing by Fr. Rom.

Vedel's account of his procedure in constructing this chronological framework is comparatively clear and frank. The definition of the three cremation-patch groups was based on an interpretation of the total find circumstances, and the finds in the graves played an important part in this work. 'Very soon it became obvious', he writes, 'that certain artefacts usually accompany each other in the same graves, while they are never found together with certain other artefacts.' However, Vedel presented no analysis of the form and style of the artefacts. It is instead clear that the topographical conditions in the burial grounds provided a decisive stimulus to the horizon formation. Thus, Vedel observed 'that certain burial grounds or certain parts of a large burial ground only contain certain specific kinds of finds and not others'.[16] One cemetery after another proved to contain one or two of the same characteristic constellation of finds. Thus cremation-patch groups 1 and 2 were represented by clearly delimited find contexts at individual burial grounds. When they appeared at the same site they were not inter-mingled but appeared then as units topographically clearly demarcated from each other. Vedel attached particular importance to the large burial ground at Kannikegaard, where material belonging to the first group was concentrated in the north-eastern part, finds from the second group were collected in the central part, and finds from the third group were recovered in the southern part.[17]

The classification procedure was accordingly a *horizoning and contrasting combination method*, in which the most important observation was the fact that the different units were so clearly separated spatially both within one cemetery and in several different cemeteries.

Once Vedel had defined the different groups, he had no difficulty in arranging them in their correct chronological order. The cairn group had its roots in the late Bronze Age. As regards the time sequence between the cairns and cremation-patch group 1, Vedel explicitly pointed out that they were directly associated by stratigraphical, topo-graphical and other find circumstances; group 1 must accordingly be the earliest group. The material of group 3, on the other hand, showed similarities with that from the great bog finds and must consequently be later than the other two groups, in which Vedel found no or very little Roman influence. Group 2 thereby fell naturally into place as the intermediate group.[18]

However, as an argument for the placing of the intermediate group, Vedel states – besides the fact that in the Kannikegaard burial ground it was situated between the other two – that it also contained 'scattered artefacts of both the other groups'.[19] Thus, here there is also an element of *grading combination dating*, which links together in a relative chronology the three type horizons established by *grouping combination method* and by *burial-ground chorology*. On the other hand, no traces of any grading analogy are to be seen in Vedel's argumentation.

Descriptive typology again
Once the chronological order had been established by this means, Vedel found it con-firmed by the fact that it did not reveal any sharp boundaries between the groups, as regards the artefacts.[20] Vedel observed that there was some kind of similarity between the artefact types of the different groups, and he realized that there was a time-

dependent change, a development, underlying this phenomenon. Now and then this found expression in a *descriptive typology*, when Vedel described in clear, evolutionary terms the course of events which he saw behind the variations in the material. Here, as an example, an extract of Vedel's discussion of the pottery:

> Thus, in the earthenware vessels too, a definite *progressive development* may be traced . . . in addition, the small vessels *begin* . . . to become more common . . . but *gradually*, as the belt hooks and the fibulae with the tips bent backwards *give place* to the ribbon-shaped and humpy fibulae, the coarse potsherds *disappear* and well-fired, medium-sized vessels *begin to appear*, followed by both vases and large vessels with several lugs, in connection with which the appearance of the small vessels *is improved* . . . at the same time as the older forms of the fibulae are to some extent *superseded*, there seems to occur a *deterioration* in the manufacture of the earthenware vessels. The workmanship *becomes less careful*, the colours dark grey, the firing *poorer* and the decorations *less exact*, in connection with which *the old forms* are partially set aside. This *development* can be traced further ahead through the inhumation graves, but the material for the observations runs out too quickly to enable *the further course* to be followed up for long. (My italics.)

By way of summary of the three groups of finds, Vedel writes in a different connection that they '*gradually merge into each other in a series of intermediate shapes*'.[21]

At this juncture, there is again reason to direct the reader's attention to the appearance of the descriptive typology in a connection in which no traces of dating by means of a grading analogy, i.e. grading typology, can be seen. Of course, one cannot exclude the possibility that Vedel also was somewhat influenced by Hans Hildebrand's typological vocabulary, which was flowering in the first section of *Towards a History of the Fibula*, which appeared in 1872, and which Vedel had read. Notwithstanding this, it is quite clear that the descriptive typology in Vedel's work (as well as in Worsaae's earlier work on Bronze Age burials, see p. 44ff.) was essentially born out of an increasingly detailed, chronological division arrived at by quite different means of dating. Another early example of descriptive typology will be found in the field of numismatics (see p. 99ff.). Descriptive typology which certainly appeared before classical evolutionary typology, i.e. grading analogy, made its entrance as an independent method of relative dating must be regarded as one of the many background elements from which evolutionary typology was formed.

NOTES

1 See p. 17ff.
2 N. G. Bruzelius 1860, pp. 30f. and 73ff.
3 Montelius 1869a, pp. 11–26.
4 von Sacken 1868, pp. 144f.
5 Montelius 1869a, pp. 6ff.
6 Keller 1858.
7 Montelius 1869a, pp. 5f., 17f.
8 H. Hildebrand 1872–80, pp. 87–142 (chapters 1–5 appeared in 1872 and chapters 6–11 in 1873).

9 H. Hildebrand 1876, p. 599.
10 Tischler 1885, p. 157.
11 Vedel 1870 and 1872. Cf. 1873.
12 Vedel 1870, pp. 56ff., 1872, pp. 20ff. and 93ff., and 1873, pp. 28f., 50ff.
13 Vedel 1872, pp. 82ff., 87f., and 1873, pp. 46ff.
14 H. Hildebrand 1872–80.
15 Vedel 1872, pp. 20ff., 52ff., 75ff., and 1873, pp. 22, 42f., 49f.
16 Vedel 1873, p. 17.
17 Vedel 1870, pp. 50ff., and 1872, pp. 51f., 55ff.
18 Vedel 1872, pp. 20ff., 59ff.
19 Vedel 1872, p. 59.
20 Vedel 1870, p. 53, and 1872, pp. 51f.
21 Vedel 1872, pp. 51f.

10

The Roman Iron Age:
the division into two periods

In 1874 the young Dane Sophus Müller published a paper entitled *A Chronology of the Early Iron Age Finds in Denmark* where he tackled the part of the early Iron Age to which the 'Roman' artefacts could be assigned, i.e. the period between the great bog finds and the pre-Roman stage. As the work of a beginner it was a considerable scientific achievement. Its simple, disciplined form and rigorously logical structure lends it a special intellectual beauty. In addition it can be regarded as more accessible for analysis than many modern works in the chronological genre.[1]

For his chronological targets, Müller selected three groups of archaeological finds, namely *fibulae*, *wine ladles* and large *bronze vessels*, in that order of importance. On account of its numerous occurrence among the finds and its continuously changing form and appearance, the fibula had at an early date become esteemed as particularly useful for chronological studies. Accordingly, Müller began his analysis with a grouping and a chronological classification of the fibulae; this classification was then used for the further division of the Roman Iron Age in Denmark. For Müller's purpose, therefore, the first parts of Hans Hildebrand's *Towards a History of the Fibula* (1872–80) had been published at an opportune time.[2]

As the first step, Müller grouped the fibulae according to their appearance in six 'forms'. However, he found no support for the dating of these fibula groups in Hildebrand's book. Hildebrand had not succeeded in 'establishing a more specific chronological relationship between the different forms'. In Müller's opinion, the reason for this was that Hildebrand 'did not make use of the testimony of the finds themselves'. Müller, however, intended to start from the particular find circumstances: 'We shall address ourselves to the burial finds, in order to seek a definite answer there.' He had already clearly described his basic chronological approach in the introduction to his paper: 'The burial finds . . . seem to provide the most reliable evidence as to the synchronism of different forms.' It was accordingly the find combinations which Müller tended to make the basis of his chronological division.

The result of Müller's examination of the burial finds, as far as the fibulae are concerned, may be summarized in his own words: 'Fibulae of forms 1 and 2 are never found in graves together with those of forms 3–6; on the other hand, many finds indicate that the latter are synchronous.' 'Moreover, the character and the ornamentation distinguish forms 1 and 2 from forms 3–6.'

The next step was to establish which of the two groups of fibulae was the earlier and which the later. For this purpose Müller made a study trip to the major continental museums which held Roman and Germanic antiquities. He then found that his fibula forms 1 and 2 had counterparts in the Roman provinces, while forms 3–6 had been common in the Germanic countries. With the tacit premiss that the direction of innovation had been from south to north, Müller concluded that 'forms 1 and 2 are the earlier and forms 3–6 the later'. This division was confirmed by finds containing forms 1 and 2 together with pre-Roman artefacts, and finds containing forms 3–6 together with artefacts dating from the middle Iron Age.

The geographic distribution of the fibulae confirmed the results of the study of find combinations; ' . . . form 1, which was accepted to be the oldest, has the most limited distribution area, form 2 extends somewhat further, and groups 3–6 are distributed even to the parts of Scandinavia which seem the last to have been strongly influenced by Roman culture'.

As regards burial customs, Müller started from the observations by Vedel and others that cremation was the predominant custom during the earliest period of the Iron Age and that inhumation did not become general until a somewhat more advanced period. Müller's fibula grouping fitted well into this pattern: 'Form 1 belongs essentially to the period when cremation was still predominant, form 1*a–c* to the transitional period, and forms 3–6 to a time when inhumation had become common.' The same observation was also made in the German material.

If, at this point, we look back at Müller's way of arranging his fibula groups in their chronological order, we find that the decisive proof was based mainly on a horizoning and contrasting combination method but that also a grading combination method was used.

The fibula grouping became the fixed basis to which the other artefacts, especially the wine ladles, strainers and bronze vessels, to a large extent came to be related.

Fig. 26. Sophus Müller (1846–1934), Danish archaeologist, in his younger days.

On the basis of their form and technical qualities, Müller divided the wine ladles and strainers into three groups which he described in detail. Once again he extracted the decisive information from the find contexts: 'forms 1 and 2 are synchronous, while neither of them has been found with form 3'. He noted that in no single instance had a strainer been found together with ladles of form 1, which were, however, known in hundreds of examples, chiefly within the frontiers of the Roman Empire. The direct opposite was the case as regarded form 3. Müller knew of these 'only from the frontier districts of the Roman Empire and from the non-Roman countries, always accompanied by a strainer'. Ladles and strainers of form 1 often carried the maker's trade-mark, but not those of form 3. Just as in the case of the fibulae, the distribution picture of the wine ladles led Müller to assume that form 1 must be older than form 3.

He then made use of combination finds with fibulae. It transpired that ladles of forms 1 and 2 had *always* been found together with fibulae of the early group and ladles of form 3 with later forms of fibula.

Müller then went on to study large, bronze vessels with hangers and divided them according to the appearance of the hanger and foot into two distinct forms. 'It may seem that these differences are unimportant, but nevertheless features from one form are never transferred to the other.' The analysis of the distribution yielded results similar to those for the fibulae and the ladles: form 1 must be older than form 2, which, unlike form 1, had been encountered only in the Roman provinces and in neighbouring regions beyond. A more reliable proof of this could be obtained only 'from a comparison with other artefacts', by which Müller meant the combination finds with the fibulae and the ladles.

After having in this way built up, step by step, a relative chronology for three important categories of artefacts and laid the foundation for 'the distinction between an early and a late period within the "Roman" Iron Age in Denmark', Müller went on to transfer the results 'to other kinds of artefacts from this period'. He did this by examining find combinations in which other groups of objects or phenomena occurred together with fibulae, wine ladles and bronze vessels.

As far as the absolute dating of the two main chronological groups was concerned, Müller solved the problem simply by dividing the four centuries available into two equal halves – the first and the second and the third and the fourth centuries A.D.

Müller's division of the Roman Iron Age into two periods is, as we have seen, based in all essentials on the *type-grounding, combination method*, with minor elements of the *grading combination method* and the use of historically known facts. Judging by Müller's very clear account of his work, grading type analogy was not employed at all.

Thus, in this masterly analysis, Müller produced for Denmark, and in practice for much larger regions, a division of the archaeological material from the Roman period: a period whose internal chronology had previously, been shrouded in mystery. Since then the find material has increased enormously and Müller's results have naturally been modified. However, they are, broadly speaking, still valid. The importance of Müller's work cannot be overestimated. It came to form the basis of all subsequent research on this period in northern Europe.

In Müller's work we encounter a comparatively detailed, chronological division based on a study of find circumstances. It is not possible to achieve this without a corresponding precision of type analysis. It may be said that Müller's work in this way represents a distinct step forward in the development of chronological methods. It was especially on this point, the more sophisticated and precise type analysis, that the young, new generation of professional archaeologists such as Hans Hildebrand, Oscar Montelius and Sophus Müller differed from the older generation to which Worsaae and his contemporaries belonged.

NOTES

1 Müller 1874.
2 H. Hildebrand 1872–80.

11

Coins and Iron Age chronology

Before leaving the subject of Iron Age chronology, I shall briefly touch upon its relationship to early numismatics. It will have become clear in the preceding pages that coins and objects dated by finds of coins were of great importance for the basic chronological stratification of the Iron Age which Worsaae, Engelhardt and Müller, *inter alios*, brought about. In his *Primeval Antiquities of Denmark* (1834), Worsaae showed that he already understood the chronological significance of the different coin groups.[1] In that respect, he was certainly influenced by his teacher, Thomsen, who was himself a numismatist. Thomsen had already presented, in the *Guide to Northern Archaeology* (1836), a simple grouping of the most important coin classes associated with the Iron Age and had demonstrated very clearly his understanding of the importance of coins for archaeological chronology.[2] Nils Gustaf Bruzelius also realized vaguely the chronological importance of coins.[3]

Bror Emil Hildebrand, the outstanding figure in Swedish numismatics in the nineteenth century, seems to have been indirectly influenced by Thomsen as early as 1829 in his doctoral thesis *Numismata Anglo-Saxonica*.[4] For the purposes of this thesis, Hildebrand had taken over the unfinished work of the deceased Sven Hylander, on which, in his turn, Thomsen had, to all appearances, had a considerable scholarly influence. Hildebrand himself afterwards came into direct contact with Thomsen and moreover in 1830 classified coins in Copenhagen under Thomsen's personal supervision.[5]

Hildebrand also soon expressed his realization of the great value of the coins for dating the native artefacts and ancient remains of the Iron Age.[6] He also made a preliminary classification of the more important groups of coins.[7] He later presented this classification of the Scandinavian coin finds into four main classes in a more detailed form in his pioneering work *Anglo-Saxon Coins Found in Swedish Soil* (1846). In this work, the coin finds were distributed into the following four main classes: (1) the *Roman* class (denarii), (2) the *Roman and Byzantine* class (solidi), (3) the *Cufic* class (Arabic silver coins dating from the eighth to tenth centuries (most of them from the period A.D. 890–955), and (4) the *Anglo-Saxon and German* class (including Scandinavian and eastern-European coins), dating from the middle of the tenth century to c. A.D. 1100.[8]

This grouping of the different inflows of imported coins during the Iron Age became an important starting-point for the Swedish archaeologists' endeavours during the latter half of the nineteenth century to get a clearer idea of the Iron-Age chronology. In this connection, both Hans Hildebrand and Montelius testified, both in words and in deeds, to their dependence on the coin finds and on Bror Emil Hildebrand's grouping of the coin inflows.[9]

Montelius' doctoral thesis, *From the Iron Age* (1869), consists of several mutually independent parts. It includes a complete catalogue of all known Scandinavian finds of coins and bracteates dating from before the Viking period. These coins represent the first two classes in Bror Emil Hildebrand's grouping, and Montelius divides them into three main groups: (1) coins dating from the early Roman Imperial period (29 B.C. to A.D. 235, chiefly denarii), (2) coins dating from the late Roman Imperial period (A.D. 235–395, mainly aurei) and (3) late-Roman and Byzantine coins (A.D. 395–518, practically entirely solidi). In addition, there are some small groups: Greek coins, Roman coins dating from before the reign of Augustus, Byzantine coins dating from the period 518–850 and finally an early Viking-period find containing Anglo-Saxon coins.[10]

No general commentary is devoted to this coin catalogue in the text, and the catalogue is used to only a very small extent in the survey which is, of course, mainly concerned with that part of the Iron Age which had no coin finds, i.e. the very earliest part. One wonders what the purpose of this list of coins really was. It is true that in his early days Montelius had been tutored in numismatics by Bror Emil Hildebrand, but he was not and never became a numismatist in the true sense, like Hans Hildebrand. He does not give the coins any numismatic treatment, nor is there any indication that it was the coins, as such, that inspired him to carry out the herculean work which went into the preparation of these lists.

What distinguishes the catalogue is instead the careful account of the circumstances of each coin find, which includes information about the find-place, the date when the

Fig. 27. Bror Emil Hildebrand (1806–84), Swedish numismatist and archaeologist.

find was made, the type of coin, its condition and secondary treatment, and finally the artefacts which may have accompanied it. In other words, throughout the catalogue the information given is of importance if the coin-finds are primarily regarded as a source of chronological knowledge. Montelius' coin catalogue gives a clear impression that its main purpose was to be used in the preparation of a more detailed, chronological analysis of the antiquities and ancient remains of the Iron Age on the basis of a vertical scale of find horizons dated by means of coins.[11] However, Montelius continued for several years to report new finds of coins in catalogue form.[12]

Thus, even in his first work, Montelius demonstrates his endeavour to underpin his chronological investigations with a long-term inventory of all the material relevant to the question. He applied this basic view with a consistency and systematization which were both the weakness and the strength of his research. His aim was always to take into account all the available material, placing special emphasis on collective finds and on find circumstances in general. In *From the Iron Age*, he introduces a more open system of reporting in Scandinavian archaeology, which is expressed in several of his early chronological works; generally speaking, this endeavour usually appears chiefly in works which, in a chronological respect, are greatly dependent on the find contexts.

In this connection, mention should also be made of Carl Tornberg's classification of the finds of Arabic coins in *Numi cufici* (1848).[13] Together with *Anglo-Saxon Coins*, this book promoted the isolation of a special material of artefacts dating from the Viking period and the division of this material into an early and a late chronological group.[14] It is difficult not to read into it a connection between Hans Hildebrand's statement of principle in 1881 about the possibility of dividing the antiquities of the Viking period into three chronological groups with the aid of the coins which accompany the brooches in the finds[15] and the division of the material of Gotland fibulae which he had made shortly before.[16] However, it should be observed that there were also considerable possibilities of chronologically dividing the material dating from the last part of the Iron Age in an indirectly historical way, as Sophus Müller did at the same period by his fundamental analysis of its various styles.[17]

NOTES

1 Worsaae 1843, pp. 52ff.
2 Thomsen 1836, pp. 80ff. Cf. chapter 4.
3 N. G. Bruzelius 1853, pp. 47f. and 79f.
4 B. E. Hildebrand 1829.
5 B. Hildebrand 1937–8, pp. 561ff., and 1934, p. 266.
6 B. E. Hildebrand 1842.
7 B. E. Hildebrand 1844, pp. 14ff.
8 B. E. Hildebrand 1846, pp. vi ff.
9 H. Hildebrand 1866, pp. 18ff. and 73ff., 1869a, p. 225, 1870, pp. 52ff., 1872b, pp. 6f., 1872a, pp. 29ff. and 195ff.; Montelius 1872a, pp. 22f., and 1878, pp. 1ff. Cf. 1884b, p. 331, 1887, pp. 240ff., and 1915, pp. 45f.
10 Montelius 1869a, pp. 31–66.
11 Cf. Åberg 1943, p. xv.

12 Montelius 1872d, 1873b and 1874a.
13 Tornberg 1848.
14 Montelius 1873c, pp. 192ff., and 1892, p. 157; H. Hildebrand 1877, pp. 501f., and 1879, pp. 49ff. and 163ff.
15 H. Hildebrand 1881, pp. 19f.
16 H. Hildebrand 1877, pp. 501f., and 1879, pp. 49ff. and 163ff.
17 Müller 1880.

Dating in the Bronze Age
with special reference to Scandinavia

After his disputation for the doctorate in 1869, Montelius for more than 15 years concentrated on the task of trying to draw up a detailed chronology for the Bronze Age of Scandinavia and to establish its absolute time-span. The final result of this enormous labour appeared in 1885 under the title of *Om tidsbestämning inom bronsåldern med särskild hänsyn till Skandinavien* (*Dating in the Bronze Age, with Special Reference to Scandinavia*).[1]

All research must be judged against its contemporary background. In this perspective, Montelius' *Dating in the Bronze Age* stands out as a unique performance. It belongs to the small group of select classics in archaeological literature, and the only reason so little attention has been paid to it by the historians of research would seem to be that it was published in Swedish (except for a French résumé of five pages) and thereby remained inaccessible to most of them.

Few research results stand out as decisive and definitive as *Dating in the Bronze Age*. It is still, after a century, fresh and topical and its conclusions are, in all essentials, still valid. Few works in archaeology, least of all in the chronological field, have had such a

Fig. 28. Oscar Montelius (1843–1921), Swedish archaeologist, in his younger days.

penetrating power and so lasting an influence. The fact that the chronology presented is, in all essentials, still in use is also a sufficient reason for us to try to find out the methodological grounds on which this work is based.

Montelius himself has, in different connections, given rather contradictory pictures of his chronological method of working. There is, however, a strong tradition that Montelius to a large extent built up his Bronze Age chronology by evolutionary typology. Typical is the following statement: 'The division of the Bronze Age into periods which was created by Oscar Montelius was based on a strictly typological grouping of artefacts',[2] or 'The book reads like a manifesto for the typological method'.[3] However, there is a conspicuous absence of typological arguments for the division into periods in this work, and the current descriptions or reproductions of typological-development series and sequences are lacking, for which reason it has also been argued that the Bronze Age periods were not a result of typology but mainly of studies of find combinations.[4] It should be mentioned that Montelius himself explains the absence of typological argumentation by saying that 'detailed accounts of the typological investigations have already or will soon be given in other places'.[5] This is, however, a highly qualified truth. Let us see what the book itself can tell us.

The material used
Owing to the unusually careful account of the material used *Dating in the Bronze Age* is much more suitable for methodological investigation than most of the other, contemporary, archaeological works, including many of Montelius' other works, both earlier and later. Montelius asserted that in this book he had reported 'the contents of *all* the finds that are known in Scandinavia and that are important in considering this question . . . ' and that 'no find that is important in considering this question and is also *reliable* has been ignored'. The lists of the closed finds contained all the finds which Montelius knew of which contained 'at least two artefacts of characteristic types' or such a characteristic type found in a grave together with unburnt or burnt bones.[6] In all, the book includes 342 such dating find-combinations from Scandinavia, of which 216 are pure artefact combinations with type-determined artefacts.

The actual type description is concerned with nine main categories of artefacts, numbered I–IX.[7] Montelius designates the most important types in each of these groups by capital letters, for example, IVA, IXE, etc. Other, less common types or those which he regarded as less important are designated by small Roman or Greek letters. Altogether, 100 types are distinguished in this way, of which 92 are reproduced in the plates. In addition, there are 35 types of other categories, which do not occur in the type descriptions but which are to be found in the tabular lists of the finds and which are also reproduced in the plates. A further four, undescribed types are reported in the find tables, where they are marked by two capital letters (for example, IIICD); Montelius seems to have regarded them as intermediate forms. Moreover, one observes four variants[8] described as 'late'; they are not reproduced but occur in the find tables. Thus, in order to obtain a complete picture of the type contents in *Dating in the Bronze Age* it is necessary to study the type descriptions on pp. 52–76, the tabular list of the contents of the periods on pp. 82–3, Appendices C–H with the tabular lists of the closed finds on pp. 270–311 and finally plates nos. 1–6. Altogether, the book deals with 144 different artefact types, of which 142 are distributed into periods.

In addition, Montelius includes special lists of all the known fibulae within and outside Scandinavia, together with the belt boxes, cups and hanging vessels, which are extremely important types of artefact for Bronze Age chronology. Thus, Appendix A includes 571 fibulae, of which 242 are continental (almost exclusively German), and Appendix B includes 247 belt boxes, cups and hanging vessels, of which 79 are continental (they also are mainly German). These lists report not only type determinations but also find places, information about the assemblage and references to the literature (in all, a compilation running to 64 pages).[9] Altogether, the account of the finds covers 133 pages, excluding the plates.

Montelius' presentation of the background material for *Dating in the Bronze Age* has no counterpart in contemporary archaeological literature and makes it possible to get an idea later of the extent to which the find combinations and other find contexts were at his disposal when he formulated the six Bronze Age periods.

Among the artefacts in the 216 artefact combinations, Montelius distinguished in various ways 144 types, of which 142 were assigned to periods.[10] Of these 142 types, 126 were found in find combinations with other types assigned to periods. However, types which were located in isolated combinations[11] are to be deducted from this figure. This leaves 122 types marked in dating combinations of artefacts.

Table 2 shows that only 20 of the 122 types assigned to periods, i.e. 14 per cent, were not located in dating combinations and that a good half of them (11) date from period 6. As regarded the other periods, the number of types not found in dating combinations was negligible, varying between 1 and 3. The state of affairs for the four central periods

Fig. 29. Sophus Müller, at a mature age. Müller, in the late 1870s and the early 1880s, raised opposition against Montelius' preparatory works on Bronze Age chronology.

Table 2. *The number of types and find combinations in the different periods, according to* Tidsbestämning

	Period						
	1	2	3	4	5	6	1–6
Combinations	4	52	47	38	68	7	216
Types	13	29	24	32	29	18	145
Types in combinations	11	28	22	29	28	7	125
Types without combinations	2	1	2	3	1	11	20
Percentage of types in combinations	85	97	93	91	96	39	86

Table 3. *Number of find combinations per type in each period*

	Period						
	1	2	3	4	5	6	1–6
Average	1	5.7	5.5	3.9	8	1	3.2
Median	1	4	4	3	5	0.5	3

2–5, to which 95 per cent of all find combinations belong, is particularly striking; the proportion of types which were found in dating combinations for these four periods is between 91 and 97 per cent.[12]

Table 3 shows the average number of find combinations per type within each period. The four central periods are well provided for also in this respect; the average number of find combinations per type varies between 3.9 and 8 or a median of between 3 and 5.

In my book *Relative Dating* (1974), figures 18–23 show, period by period, how the types which occur in dating artefact finds are combined with each other. They also provide information as to the number of combinations for each type, the number of other types with which the type in question is associated in combinations, and the number of times specimens of the types have been discovered together with other types. The hanging-vessel type IXE (period 5) has the highest numbers. It appeared in 39 finds, combined on 115 occasions with 22 other types within the period (also combined on seven occasions with four types from other periods). (Figs. 30a–b below.)

Finally, figures 31–2 below show the types for which periods have been given and which have also been located in combinations which contain types assigned to other periods. However, all except three of these types have at the same time been located in a number of finds which is adequate to fix them clearly within the given period. Of these types, there is, however, only one which lacks a majority of finds within its own period, namely the bracelet type VIL, which, together with the fibula type VIIe,[13] is the only type which Montelius seems to have dated against the evidence of the find combinations. He has put type VIIe in period 4, although it is combined – in only one find, it is true – with three period-3 types. He assigns type VIL to period 6, in spite of the fact

		IC	D	E	F	IIA	IIIA	B	e	IVA	VA	α	VID	VIIA	a	b	c	VIIIA	B	C	D	fig26	27	28	29	30	31	33	41	21
flanged axe	I C	7·7·1																												
axe with stop-ridge	,, D	1	10·10·3																											
,,	,, E	1	1	33·16·13																										
,,	,, F	1	1	2	21·15·6																									
socketed axe	II A	1	1	1	1	9·9·2																								
sword	III A		1		1		6·5·4																							
,,	,, B	1	1	11	2	1		58·23·22																						
,,	,, e					1			2·2·1																					
razor	IV A			1			1	2		11·7·4																				
neck-ring	V A							1			5·5·1																			
neck ornament	α				1			2				43·13·16																		
arm-ring	VI D											2	10·7·4																	
brooch	VII A			2				4		1		2	1	16·11·6																
,,	,, a				1			1							3·3·1															
,,	,, b			1				1				1		1		5·5·2														
,,	,, c							2			1						8·6·3													
tutulus	VIII A				1			5			1	8	1				2	43·14·14												
belt ornament	,, B				2			2			1	11	3	1			1	9	42·14·14											
tutulus	,, C			1				2			1	6	1	1		1	1	4	4	27·14·9										
doomed button	,, D			2	1	1	1	4	1	3		5		1				3	3	1	36·18·11									
chape	fig 26							1					1					1				3·3·2								
,,	,, 27							1													1		4·4·1							
belt hook	,, 28		1	2	2		2	5		1		1	1		1			2	1		2		1	25·14·9						
spear-head	,, 29	1	1	1	1	1		1																	7·7·1					
,,	,, 30	1	1	3	3	1		2				1						2	1	1	1				1	20·13·5				
sickle	,, 31			1	1							2						3	2	2	1					2	15·9·4			
tweezers	,, 33		1	2				4		2				1			1				4		1	3				21·10·8		
double button	,, 41			1				2				1		1				1	1	1	1						1	2	12·10·3	
shaft-hole axe	,, 21																													

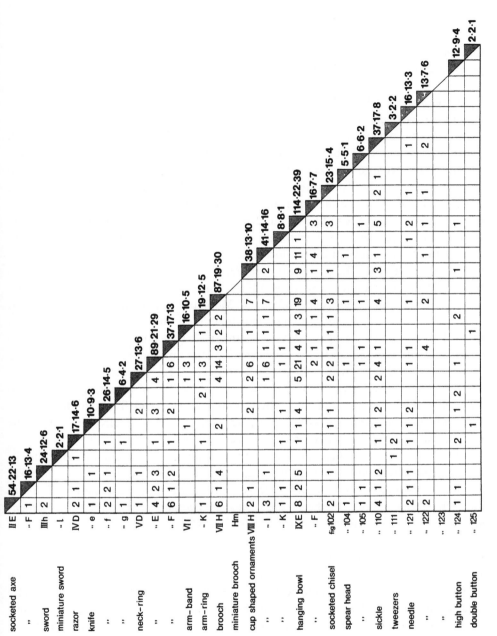

Figs. 30a–b. Grid diagrams for periods 2 and 5, based on information presented in Montelius' *Dating in the Bronze Age* of 1885. In the oblique row of numbers, the figure to the right specifies the total number of combinations for the type in question; the central figure specifies the number of types and the left figure the number of artefacts, with which the type is combined. For both periods, most finds are firmly tied to period by a sufficient number of combinations. The same is the case with the other periods. Montelius, therefore, can have had no difficulties in establishing his six time horizons merely on the basis of find combinations. (After Gräslund 1974, figs. 19 and 22.)

that the finds almost tip the scales in favour of period 5 (find assemblage 10–8–2 for period 5 and 7–4–2 for period 6).[14]

Find-combination chronology

If, for the time being, we disregard period 6, it would consequently seem to be possible to state that the division into periods could, in all essentials, have been carried out with the aid of all the find combinations which Montelius so carefully listed. These combinations would seem to have constituted the basis for the actual period grouping, the horizoning stage in the investigation. The chronological order of the six periods, finally, was also simple and was quite achievable in virtue of these find combinations. No less than 40 of the types link together periods 2–6 through mixed finds, as figures 31–3 show. In some cases, different specimens of the same type actually link together no less than three periods. Thus, the knife type IV*a* connects period 3 with both periods 2 and 4, and the socketed axe type IIE, the torque type VE, the gold bracelet type VIK, the fibula type VIIH and the hanging vessel type IXE all connect period 5 with both periods 4 and 6.[15] (This circumstance does not conflict with Montelius' statement that 'no known find contains objects *characteristic* of two periods that do not follow each other'.)[16] Objects that belong to the same category of types are the sickle (fig. 110), the tweezers (fig. 111) and the double-button (fig. 125), whose find circumstances (see figs. 21–2) led Montelius to assign them to both period 4 and period 5.[17] All these types, which in various ways overlapped periods, afforded the possibility of arranging periods 2–6 chronologically with the aid of the grading combination method. Through the period-1 finds, which showed contacts with the last part of the Stone Age, finally, the whole of the relative chronological sequence would have been given.

By way of summary, I may say that it was quite possible for Montelius to group, in all essentials, the Scandinavian Bronze-Age material in periods 1–5 by the *grouping, find-combination method* and to link together chronologically at least periods 2–6 and indirectly periods 1 and 2 by the *grading combination method, without using the evolutionary analysis by which Montelius himself described his typology*.

General evidence of the finds

It is to be noted that, in this investigation, I have not taken into account all the possibilities of dating or chronological guidance which Montelius had at his disposal by means of no less than 126 other combinations listed in *Dating*, namely those which consisted of only *one* characteristic artefact in combination with information about a characteristic form of grave. These are reported in Appendices C–H under the heading of 'Find circumstances'. I have paid equally little attention to all the artefacts whose types Montelius did not determine; they are of about 30 different categories, listed in the Appendices under the heading of 'Miscellaneous items', which may also have contributed information on the question. Nor have I paid any attention to the many border-line cases, which Montelius placed within parentheses ( ) or commented on specially in the text.

As I shall show below, it would probably have been fairly simple for Montelius to assign also most of the 20 types which were not included in dating artefact combinations to a period on the basis of find evidence of another kind. In this connection, we have a certain amount of guidance also from his earlier writings on the Bronze Age.

The 20 types are as follows (the references are to the figures in *Dating*). *Period 1*: type III*b*, palstave (fig. 6), and the type shown in fig. 3, massive shaft-hole axe; *period 2*: the type shown in fig. 21, shaft-hole axe with spiral ornamentation; *period 3*: the fibula types VIID (fig. 70) and VIICD; *period 4*: type III*g*, flange-hilted sword, type III*k*, miniature sword (fig. 76), and type VII*e*, fibula; *period 5*: type VII*Hm*, miniature spectacle fibula (fig. 129); type IV*h*, crescent-shaped razor (fig. 131), types VI (fig. 134) and VH, torques, type V*c*, 'Kronenhalsring' (crown torque) (fig. 136), type VII*α*, 'tutulus-shaped' fibula (fig. 143), type IXF, hanging vessel of 'late' type, and the pin types shown in figs. 137 and 139–42.

Let us begin with the palstave, for which Montelius had, in point of fact, access to closed artefact combinations, namely the extra-Scandinavian ones. When, a few years previously, he published the Pile find – which forms the nucleus of his period 1 – he also discussed the palstave chronologically. As authority for dating them to the period of the Pile find, the earliest period of the Bronze Age, he then referred explicitly to two combination finds in Mecklenburg. In one case, a flanged axe was accompanied by a wide, bronze bracelet of the Pile type and, in the other, by three such bracelets, a flanged axe and five daggers.[18] Accordingly, he dated type III*b* to the initial period of the Bronze Age, clearly with the support of the find contexts.

Basically, the miniature fibula type VII*Hm* can also be regarded as being dated by combination. It is quite clear that Montelius regarded it as being, apart from its size, identical in type with the spectacle fibula type VIIH, which is firmly fixed by numerous finds in period 5.[19]

Montelius would seem to have been in a position simply to group several of the other types into periods through finds connected with a characteristic burial custom of the kind which he regarded as 'dating'.[20] We then immediately find that the fibula type VIID occurs in no less than five burial finds containing burnt bones in stone coffins of less than full length, precisely those which characterize the transitional custom of cremation in period 3. One of these burial finds also includes type VIICD. As, at the same time, they are lacking in period-2 and period-3 combinations, there cannot have been any alternative other than assignment to period 3. The types for which the associated burial custom would seem to have constituted dating evidence include also the different types of pin illustrated in fig. 137 (with a double-spiral head), fig. 139 (with a single-spiral head) and figs. 140–2 (swan's-neck pins of different designs). Montelius remarks that these types are found together with burnt bones, 'either lying in an earthenware vessel or in a "cremation patch"'; for the latter form of grave, he refers to Vedel's finds on Bornholm.[21] As Montelius had already, a few years previously, clearly marked his view that Vedel's cremation patches were a transitional form of grave between the end of the Bronze Age and the beginning of the Iron Age,[22] he probably did not feel any hesitation in stating period 6 as the chronological address of the pin types. Moreover, he knew very well that swan's-neck pins made of iron also existed.[23]

As regards the ordinary pin with a spiral head (fig. 139), its assignment to period 6 would also seem to have been a simple choice for Montelius, not only on account of the

Types	Per.2	Per.3	Per.4	Per.5	Per.6
IV A	11·7·4	4·4·2			
VI D	10·7·4	1·2·1			
VIII B	42·14·14	1·1·1			
III F	1·1·1	5·3·3			
IV b	1·1·1	21·10·10			
VI E	1·1·1	16·10·8			
VII B	1·1·1	29·14·12			
IV a	1·1·1	29·15·13	1·1·1		
V b		7·7·2	2·2·1		
VII C		8·7·4	1·1·1		
VII d		18·10·10	1·1·1		
fig. 65		5·4·2	1·1·1		
IX A		10·8·3	1·1·1		
VII F		1·1·1	8·7·4		
IX B		1·1·1	9·7·5		
II C			32·18·9	15·12·4	
II D			4·4·1	2·2·1	
III f			9·9·3	10·7·2	
IV C			6·4·3	6·6·1	
II F			2·2·2	16·13·4	
III h			1·1·1	24·12·6	
IV e			1·1·1	10·9·3	
IV f			1·1·1	26·14·5	
V D			2·2·1	27·13·6	
VI I			2·2·1	16·10·5	
VIII H			1·1·1	38·13·10	
fig. 102			3·2·2	23·15·4	
fig. 121			1·1·1	16·13·3	
II E			1·1·1	54·22·13	2·2·2
V E			4·3·1	89·21·29	1·1·1
VI K			3·2·2	19·12·5	1·1·1
VII H			3·2·2	87·19·30	4·1·2
IX E			5·3·3	114·22·39	4·2·1
VIII I				41·14·16	1·1·1
IX F				16·7·7	1·1·1
fig. 122				13·7·6	6·2·1
II F: 6				1·1·1	8·5·3
V G				2·2·2	10·6·5
V H				1·1·1	10·6·4
VI L				10·8·2	7·4·2

Fig. 31. No less than 40 of Montelius' types link together periods 2–6 into a chronological sequence, by their appearing in chronologically mixed finds. (For explanation of column figures, see fig. 30.) Cf. fig. 32. (After Gräslund 1974, fig. 24.)

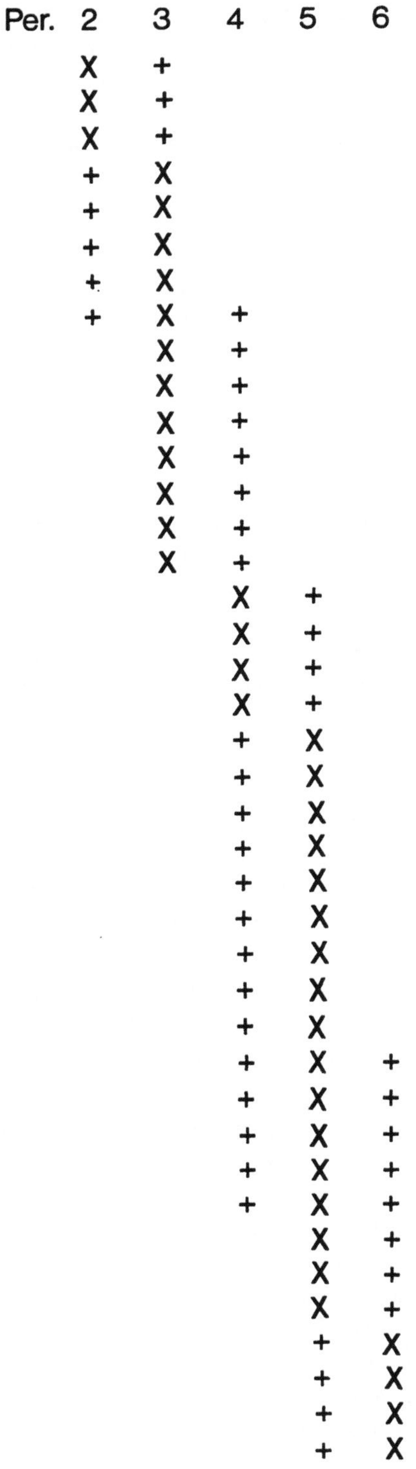

Per.	2	3	4	5	6
	X	+			
	X	+			
	X	+			
	+	X			
	+	X			
	+	X			
	+	X			
	+	X	+		
		X	+		
		X	+		
		X	+		
		X	+		
		X	+		
		X	+		
		X	+		
			X	+	
			X	+	
			X	+	
			X	+	
			+	X	
			+	X	
			+	X	
			+	X	
			+	X	
			+	X	
			+	X	
			+	X	
			+	X	+
			+	X	+
			+	X	+
			+	X	+
			+	X	+
				X	+
				X	+
				X	+
				+	X
				+	X
				+	X
				+	X

Fig. 32. Fig. 31 transferred into a simple occurrence diagram. For each type, X shows the period to which the majority of its combinations belong, while + shows the find majority. Figs. 31–2 demonstrate that the relative ordering of the six periods was easily done by means of the many finds with a chronologically mixed context. Consequently, Montelius needed no grading analogy (grading typology) to establish his Bronze Age chronology. (After Gräslund 1974, fig. 25.)

fact that he knew most of the pin types, including those with spiral heads, dated from a late period in the Bronze Age but also on account of the find circumstances on the whole. He was well aware that these spiral-headed pins, like the above-mentioned types in figs. 140–2, appeared in Silesia and in other places in northern Germany, in burial grounds which he regarded, as a whole, as being synchronous with his period 6 and the late group of graves at Hallstatt respectively.[24]

For several of the remaining types, very simple analogies would seem to have been adequate to place them in the period system. Montelius had previously found a reliable dating also for type IVh, representing crescent-shaped razors: 'That these date from the end of our Bronze Age is shown, *inter alia*, by the fact that identical iron knives have been found several times.'[25] The burial custom also indicated to Montelius a clear dating to the late Bronze Age.[26]

Other evidence

Type VIIα, the 'tutulus-shaped' fibula, actually clearly dates, like the crown torque type Vc, from the earliest part of the Iron Age. When nevertheless Montelius now assumed that it dated from the Bronze Age, he could hardly place it anywhere but in its very last period, since he had observed that the fibula's pin was always made of iron.[27] In an earlier connection, he had also observed that its bronze alloy almost corresponded to that which was common during 'the period after the end of the real Bronze Age'.[28] The crown torque, type Vc, was, in its turn, also placed in period 6[29] on account of a combination find with this fibula type.

As regards the remaining seven types, neither *Dating* nor any other of Montelius' writings seems to give any clue with regard to possible access to direct dating finds. However, as concerns the type shown in fig. 21, the large shaft-hole axe with spiral ornamentation, the spiral ornamentation, as such, was linked with period 2 by an extraordinarily large number of find combinations. The dating of the axe type was thereby self-evident and required no form and style comparison of a profound nature.

Montelius seems to have placed the shaft-hole axe (fig. 3) in period 1 chiefly on the basis of its linear triangle ornamentation.[30] Even at the beginning of the 1870s, he had completely misjudged – no doubt on account of the scarcity of Scandinavian find combinations – the chronological position of the very earliest Bronze Age finds, which he assigned to the late Bronze Age.[31] He afterwards made a discreet correction,[32] but without mentioning the shaft-hole axes, about whose dating he seems to have long been uncertain.[33] He does not discuss the earliest geometric decoration even in his paper entitled *On the Ornamentation of the Scandinavian Bronze Age*,[34] published in 1881. It was only in connection with the detailed publication of the Pile find the following year and the consequent comparison with similar finds in continental Europe[35] that Montelius became aware, through the find circumstances, that the spiral-ornamented artefacts of the early Scandinavian Bronze Age had been preceded by a chronological horizon that included special manifestations of ornamental style. As soon as the find contexts showed clearly that flat axes and flanged axes, as well as triangular daggers, dated from the initial phase of the Bronze Age and had contacts in the finds with the

Stone Age, it also became clear that the rectilinear decoration, chiefly in the form of solid triangles, which appeared on both daggers and flanged axes[36] constituted an ornamental *Leitmotiv* for the initial period of the Bronze Age. Moreover, in 1882, Montelius' complete division of the Bronze Age into periods appeared for the first time, including period 1, in several different drafts which have been preserved.[37] Thus, the background of the placing of the shaft-hole-axe type in period 1 seems to have been a simple, ornament analogy, ultimately based on the evidence of the find circumstances.

Montelius clearly interpreted the fibula type VII*e*[38] as a simpler variant with no decoration of the fibula of Bornholm type (type VII*d*, fig. 67),[39] which was securely dated by finds in period 3 in his system. Consequently, the period placing of type VII*e* did not require any detailed type analysis either but appeared almost spontaneously.

As regards the miniature sword types III*g* and III*k* (fig. 76), there was the miniature type III*i* (with a cruciform hilt), which had already been dated by combination to period 4, as a pointer to the placing of miniature swords in general; Montelius himself points to similarities with the sword type III*f* (fig. 74).[40] He had previously interpreted the torque types VI and VK (figs. 134–5), with their varied twisting of the metal rod (imitated in the decoration), as being clearly related to the other, different, torque types, with their varied, moulded twisting, and as being 'typologically connected' with them. Generally speaking, he also knew that, as a form of object, the torques were densely concentrated in the last part of the Bronze Age.[41] As regards type VK, however, he puts in the reservation that it really dates from the actual transitional period between the Bronze and the Iron Ages.[42]

Finally, the hanging-vessel type F ('late type') is not to be found either in the type description or in the plates section; it is given only in the table of the contents of the periods on p. 83. No explanation of the type designation is given anywhere; here we have to assume that Montelius made a purely 'typological' evaluation.

It has emerged here that Montelius made chronological judgments on the basis of the find contexts also as regards most of the 20 types which were not included in Scandinavian artefact combinations. Only five of these types[43] would seem to have required a somewhat more detailed comparison of similarities, and only one seems to need anything like a pure typological dating.[44]

Summary of dating evidence and method

For the great majority of the types in *Dating*, i.e. for *no less than 97 per cent of them*, Montelius actually had access to find combinations and other find contexts in producing the division of the Bronze Age into six periods. This clearly shows that *the chronological order of these periods did not require any evolutionary analysis of a typological nature* for its realization. This chronological order emanated spontaneously from the chronologically mixed finds, which were sufficient to link together all the six periods with each other and also to connect the Bronze Age with the latest part of the Stone Age and the earliest part of the Iron Age. In addition, there was the stratigraphic evidence of which, as I mentioned in chapter 7, Montelius was very well aware. It is true that he repeats also in *Dating* his customary assurance that he had begun his chronological investigation with

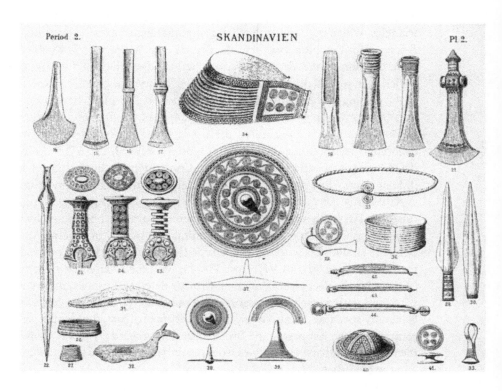

a purely typological analysis and had only afterwards checked the result by the closed finds. But, in spite of this, the book contains only very small elements of typological analysis.

For more than 15 years, Montelius recorded systematically the Bronze Age finds from practically almost all the known museum and private collections in northern Europe and 'thoroughly explored most of the collections of antiquities in central and southern Europe'.[45] As regarded the material underlying his chronology he had 'had opportunities to see for himself almost all the finds mentioned below' (i.e. in all the Appendices C–H).[46] He had mastered, as no other archaeologist had done, the complete archaeological literature within the field of Bronze-Age research. It may therefore be asserted at once – precisely as Sophus Müller pointed out with regard to the typologists' method of working even before *Dating in the Bronze Age* appeared[47] – that Montelius was quite unable to deal with the Bronze-Age material without preconceived opinions as to the chronology. Even if Montelius had – against all the evidence – deliberately tried to contract all this knowledge, in order to be able to construct a completely 'pure', typological chronology of the Bronze Age, his chances of success would have been less than those of any other of his contemporaries. Moreover, his constantly expressed assurance that 'in every typological investigation it is otherwise always necessary to study the find circumstances with the greatest care'[48] removes any suspicion in that direction.

It is noteworthy that Montelius does not say a word about his results being based on typology, when he presents them to the foreign public in the French summary. This résumé was moreover reprinted at the same time, word for word, as a separate paper in the French journal *Matériaux pour l'histoire primitive de l'homme*;[49] strangely enough, this was the only kind of circulation which *Dating in the Bronze Age* obtained outside the Scandinavian and, to a certain extent, the German sphere of archaeological research. It should also be mentioned that, on one of the few occasions when he later touched upon the method underlying his work – in a series of reminiscences presented 35 years later – Montelius clearly stresses that it was the find contexts which gave him the key to the periodization of the Bronze Age.[50]

Montelius himself summarized his Bronze Age chronology in the following words: ' . . . a large number of reliable finds are known, each of which consists exclusively of types which I have assigned to one and the same period'.[51] One would undoubtedly get nearer to the truth by using a different sequence of clauses, viz. ' . . . the periods which I have drawn up are represented by types which are known from a large number of reliable finds'.

This is not to assert that, during the long preparatory work for *Dating*, Montelius never proceeded typologically and only occasionally made purely typological analyses. Typologically arranged investigations of individual categories of object occur in several of his minor writings. As I showed in the previous chapter, however, it would seem to be clear that this typology mainly took the form of fitting artefacts into frameworks

◄ Fig. 33a–b. The main artefacts types of periods, 2 *a*, and 5, *b*, as illustrated in Montelius' *Bronze Age Chronology* 1885, Plates 2 and 5.

already sketched out by the find contexts or, in other cases, was only the expression of a descriptive typology which, in evolutionary terms, depicted a chronological order of artefacts achieved by other means. This would seem to apply also to the preparatory works for *Dating* like *The Bronze Age in Northern and Central Sweden* (1872–3), for example.[52] Another example is the paper entitled *Two Bronze-Age Finds from the Parish of Kareby*; this title conceals a 'typological' study of Bronze Age hanging vessels. At the same time, it contains an extraordinarily thorough examination of all the find circumstances for both hanging vessels, belt cups, fibulae and grooved torques.[53]

NOTES

1 Montelius 1885a. English edition, Montelius 1986.
2 Stenberger 1964, p. 185, 2nd edn 1971, p. 185; cf. Nordén 1921; Rudbeck 1943a; Arbman 1954, pp. 63, and 1969, pp. 33f.; Rosén 1966, pp. 39f.; A. Åberg 1966; Kossinna 1913a, p. 107, and 1922, pp. 313ff.; K. H. Jacob-Friesen 1928, pp. 164ff.; Daniel 1950, p. 147; G. Jacob-Friesen 1967, pp. 6, 8 and 15ff.; Filip 1966, pp. 170f.
3 Klindt-Jensen 1975, p. 88.
4 Lindqvist 1922, p. 215; Åberg 1943, pp. xvi f. and xxi f.; cf. Gjessing 1946, p. 138; B. Almgren 1967, pp. 30ff.
5 Montelius 1885a, p. 51.
6 Montelius 1885a, pp. 79, 265 and introduction.
7 Montelius 1885a, pp. 52–76: 'shaft hole axes', 'socketed axes', 'swords and daggers', 'knives', 'neck ornaments', 'bracelets', 'fibulae', 'round plates, tutuli and cups' and 'bronze boxes and hanging bowls'.
8 The letter types IIF, VIIIK, IXE and IXF.
9 Montelius 1885a, pp. 201–64.
10 However, the tutulus form VIIIEF and the fibula form VIIGH, which Montelius evidently interpreted as transitional types between periods 3 and 4 and between periods 4 and 5 respectively, were not allotted places in the system.
11 Types VIID and VIICD and types Vc and VIIα, which are included in pairs, one pair in each find. None of these types was in contact with any other datable artefact.
12 Types 110, 111 and 125 are placed in both periods 4 and 5. The total number of types is accordingly only 142 and of types in combinations 122.
13 Montelius 1885a, pp. 68 and 72.
14 Montelius 1885a, p. 83.
15 Montelius 1885a, pp. 282, 287, 302 and 311.
16 Montelius 1885a, p. 85.
17 Montelius 1885a, p. 295.
18 Montelius 1882, pp. 150f.
19 Montelius 1885a, pp. 21 and 70f.
20 Montelius 1885a, p. 265. Cf. pp. 78f. and under the heading of 'Fyndomständigheter' in Appendices C–H and also above, chapter 2.
21 Montelius 1885a, pp. 308f.; cf. 1883, p. 184.
22 Montelius 1881b, pp. 116ff.
23 Montelius 1885a, p. 308.
24 Montelius 1881b, pp. 112ff. and 156f.
25 Montelius 1881b, p. 115.
26 Montelius 1885a, p. 308.
27 Montelius 1885a, pp. 157ff.
28 Montelius 1885a, p. 160; cf. 1881b, p. 111.

29 Montelius 1885a, pp. 309f. and 323.
30 Montelius 1885a, pp. 76f., pl. 1, fig. 3a.
31 Montelius 1872a, pp. 40ff., and 1872–3, pp. 176f.
32 Montelius 1876b, p. 913, note 5.
33 Montelius 1872–3, pp. 216f., and 1880, pp. 230f.
34 Montelius 1881a.
35 Montelius 1882.
36 For example, Worsaae 1859, fig. 179; Madsen 1872, pl. 11, figs. 8 and 15.
37 Three of Montelius' handwritten drafts of a schedule of the Bronze-Age periods with the main type contents are dated '7/4/82', '10/82' and 'okt. 1882'. In them, Montelius includes also a seventh period, 'the transition to the Iron Age'. ATA. Cf. Montelius 1881b, pp. 121f., and N. Åberg 1943, pp. xxiv f.
38 Montelius 1885a, p. 72.
39 See Vedel 1878, p. 85, pl. 1:1.
40 Montelius 1885a, pp. 59f.
41 Montelius 1881b, pp. 100ff.
42 Montelius 1885a, p. 65.
43 The period-3 types III*g* and III*k* and the period-6 types VI, VK and IXF ('late').
44 The hanging-vessel type IXF ('late').
45 Montelius 1885a (preface with no heading).
46 Montelius 1885a, p. 266.
47 Müller 1884, pp. 175ff.
48 Montelius 1903, p. 17; cf. 1884a, p. 3, and 1899, p. 265.
49 Montelius 1885b.
50 Montelius 1919.
51 Montelius 1885a, p. 84.
52 Montelius 1872–3.
53 Montelius 1877b.

13

Montelius' own account of his chronological method

Montelius described his chronological method partly in the presentation of his chronological results and partly in separate methodological studies, such as *The Methods and Materials of the Archaeologist* (1884),[1] *Typology or the Theory of Evolution Applied to Human Labour* (1899)[2] and *Die typologische Methode (Typological Method)* (1903).[3] In one respect, however, Montelius' account is unclear: he does not give a clear-cut answer to the question of how he himself evaluates the mutual involvement of typology and the find-combination method in his own chronological method.

Montelius' most usual – and most noted – description of this state of affairs amounts to saying that he began his chronological studies by arranging the material in accordance with its own internal criteria and that it was only afterwards that he checked, with the aid of the closed finds, that the result was correct. This description is best reproduced by a few quotations:

> The circumstances which accompany the different finds thus confirm fully the opinion on the development of the types of Scandinavian hilts to which one is led by the study of the form and the ornamentation of each of these types. (1876)[4]

> That the decorative motifs which I have here assigned to the early and the late Bronze Age really date from different periods is proved, *inter alia*, by the fact that the two kinds neither occur on the same objects nor on objects which have been found together, and this is true although both kinds are common with a large part of the Scandinavian region. (1881)[5]

> This account of the relationships of the separate forms to each other with respect to age is based only on a consideration of the types themselves and of the internal characteristics for age determination which they possess. We shall now see whether the find circumstances confirm the correctness of this account . . . One would then seem to be able to say without exaggeration that this order, which is based only on internal, typological grounds, is in complete agreement with that which the find circumstances show to be the correct one. (1880–2)[6]

> The archaeologist no longer regards it as his only task to describe and compare the antiquities from different countries and to investigate life in these countries in bygone times. He nowadays tries to trace the internal connection between the types and to show how one developed from the other. We call this *typology*.

> In principle, the typological investigation is very simple. In studying a group of antiquities, one first collects as large a material as possible, arranges it in the way

which the internal criteria of the separate types seem to require and then investigates whether the circumstances under which the separate types were found confirm the correctness of the view of the mutual ages of the types which one has adopted. (1884)[7]

I first examined separately the most important series of weapons, tools, ornaments and vessels, together with their decorations, in order to get to know the course of their development and to see the order in which the types followed each other, judging by their own criteria. Then I examined the burial finds already known in the Scandinavian region and all other finds which might yield any information about the mutual ages of the separate types. (1885)[8]

In the great majority of cases, it is accordingly possible to decide, simply by considering the purely typological circumstances, which form is the earliest and which the latest. In the few cases in which this is not possible, the answer will be supplied by the find circumstances, which one should moreover always try to analyse with the greatest possible accuracy. (1899)[9]

If we compare the typological series with reliable finds, we see how all finds of this kind bear witness, with an astonishing unanimity, that the types really appear after each other in the sequence which the typological investigation induces us to assume. (1903)[10]

The passages quoted report the working methods of pure classical typology. The emphatic description, repeated almost word for word, probably reproduce Montelius' chronological method as he preferred to interpret it. However, one finds, even in the works just quoted, formulations which may be interpreted in a different way:

The relative dates of a country's antiquities can, in the great majority of cases, be obtained by studying the country's own archaeological conditions, without it being necessary to know about these conditions in other countries. For this purpose, it is necessary only that a sufficient material of reliable finds shall be available and that the archaeologist shall study attentively the contents of these finds and the circumstances under which they were made.

After describing this method of drawing chronological conclusions from the closed finds, Montelius continues: 'One also gets powerful aid in this connection from the typological investigation'. (1884)[11]

The results with respect to the ages of the separate types, to which the study of the contents of the graves has led, are confirmed by an investigation of a quite different kind, namely of the different types' relationships to and development from each other. (1885)[12]

In the last two quotations selected, Montelius has described a procedure which is the direct opposite of the one previously mentioned: first, a find-combination chronology is drawn up and, secondly, this chronology is checked by making a typological examination.

In his pamphlet attacking the 'typological' method of Hildebrand and Montelius *A Small Contribution to the Methodology of Prehistoric Archaeology* (1884), Sophus Müller had pointed out, *inter alia*, that it was impossible preliminarily to arrange the antiquities typologically without regard to the find circumstances and only afterwards to check the result by the finds. He considered, with good reason, that no scientist can put aside the knowledge which he unavoidably possesses of the find circumstances and prevent this knowledge from influencing the typological analysis:

> I would be the first to admit the value of the typologists' results and to recognize their often admirable hypotheses, but, at the same time, I would be the last to concede that these results have been gained solely by a comparison of the forms of artefacts. The typologists have used their own method only rarely and on points of purely secondary importance – and in these cases they have not reached and could not reach beyond conjecture; they generally rely, half or wholly unconsciously, on the observations of collective finds and they also let the testing of the hypotheses follow the typological treatment . . . But I would not say a word against this method, if it could be used at all. It is, however, unusable and has never been used. One cannot disregard the find observations, if there are any, and the typologists themselves have not done so . . . But why pretend that the results have emerged from a complete and independent comparison of forms, which has only afterwards been tested on the number of observations?[13]

In a supplement to *The Methods* (1884) which has seldom been commented on, Montelius gave a very brief answer to Müller's long article. In doing so, he adduced the following arguments:

> The method which the Swedish typologists use consists not only in investigating all the known archaeological artefacts and their find circumstances but also in trying to gain all the information which can be obtained by a study of the internal connections of the types. As I have shown in the preceding pages, *these two investigations should always proceed in parallel* [my italics]. In the printed account, however, one has, in order to secure order and lucidity, to describe first one side of the matter and then the other . . . In that case, it is also of little importance in which order the accounts of these two kinds of observations are given.[14]

Montelius' answer is very cautious and evasive and he does not touch upon the question of the part played by 'the observations of collective finds' in typological work.

Müller had evidently touched on a sensitive point. Having been criticized for the statement that he began his chronological analysis by arranging the material in chronological order exclusively according to its internal criteria and that he only afterwards, as a pure checking measure, examined the find circumstances, Montelius now admitted that, in actual fact, he carried out the two operations *in parallel* with each other, in other words, exactly as Müller had surmised. Retreating yet another step, Montelius explains that it was only a *coincidence* that the typological analysis was reported in print first. However, he has thereby, in fact, reduced the whole question to a completely uninteresting and purely practical matter of choice. If one is to judge from what he says, it was accordingly only a matter of *chance* that he did not present the results of the find-combination analysis first and the fruits of the typological investigation last.

It can accordingly be stated that, when, for the first and only time, he answered criticism of his methodology, Montelius reluctantly admitted that his standard account was misleading. There is therefore no reason to regard Montelius as the archaeologist who systematically kept separate typology and find-combination analysis in his chronological studies, whether we judge the question on the basis of his chronological works or on that of his methodological theory.

Over and over again, Montelius points out that the typological series are verified by the finds.[15] If there is no agreement, this may be due to the fact that a find is not 'reliable' or has been 'misunderstood'. But he usually indicates that the error may have arisen in the typological analysis. One reason may be that there is often a difference between the age of the specimen and that of the type[16] and another (as far as the type series are concerned) that 'some mistake has been made in their arrangement'.[17] When, in this way, he indicates that in principle he gave priority to the evidence of the finds, it is difficult to see anything meaningful in first carrying out a separate typological analysis and then checking the result by the finds. When there is a relatively good supply of closed finds – as there is with regard to the Bronze Age – the whole procedure is thereby reduced almost to an end in itself, an intellectual game with little more purpose than to demonstrate how the research worker has mastered the material and the method. But, after all, this was not how Montelius proceeded.

All systematic, chronological analysis, in the form of either 'typology' or the combination method, calls for type classification. But Montelius did not make separate type classifications for the different methods but carried out the same, fundamental, type analysis whether he was working typologically or with find combinations. It is certain that because the combination method requires a type analysis Montelius himself found it difficult to keep separate the different lines of thought which were doubtless always present side by side in his mind. The types of find combination also emphasize how closely united type classification and the find-combination method may be. Before a type classification has become clear, the constantly recurring types of find combination may often simplify this classification by emphasizing or drawing attention to the constant element in the material (the actual types). Although Montelius was, for his time, an unusually methodologically aware chronologist, he seems in many respects not to have been completely clear as to the different elements in his chronological constructions. This is something which is more conspicuous in his methodological theory than in his working results. He never gave any clear-cut explanation of his chronological method.

Undoubtedly, the fact that Montelius had familiarized himself with the find circumstances from the very beginning of his chronological work, as regarded both the Bronze Age and the Iron Age, contributed to his own difficulty in distinguishing between cause and effect in his chronological lines of thought and in keeping separate the elements of find-combination dating and grading type analogy. Here, we undoubtedly have a part of the explanation of the distorted picture of his own method which Montelius eventually left to posterity.

NOTES

1 Montelius 1884a.
2 Montelius 1899.
3 Montelius 1903.
4 Montelius 1876b, pp. 898f.
5 Montelius 1881a, p. 65.
6 Montelius 1880–2, pp. 81 and 123; cf. pp. 128 and 137.
7 Montelius 1884a, pp. 1ff.
8 Montelius 1885a, p. 51; cf. pp. 79, 84 and 267. Cf. 1903, p. 16f.
9 Montelius 1899, p. 265.
10 Montelius 1903, pp. 16f.
11 Montelius 1884a, pp. 17f.
12 Montelius 1885a, p. 8.
13 Müller 1884, pp. 175f.
14 Montelius 1884a, p. 25.
15 Montelius 1884a, pp. 2f., 1885a, p. 79, 1899, pp. 265f., and 1900, pp. 1ff.
16 Montelius 1884a, p. 3.
17 Montelius 1899, p. 266; cf. 1903, p. 20.

14

The origin of typology as chronological method

The early typological works of Hildebrand and Montelius

As has been pointed out, it was Hans Hildebrand who first described a typological method in scientific works.[1] At the same time, as Almgren has stressed, Hildebrand in his first 'typological' works did not demonstrate 'typological connections for chronological purposes but in order to call attention to the connections in the cultural sequence'.[2]

In Hildebrand's doctoral thesis, *The Swedish People in Heathen Times* (1866), there are a number of descriptions of the developmental connections between artefacts. However, concrete examples of a chronologically active, grading typology are entirely absent. In actual fact, this work contains rather few elements of artefact analysis. As regards datings, Hildebrand emphasizes that it is the closed finds which prove the chronological order and that, in this connection, especially, the finds of coins are of great importance (the thesis deals chiefly with the Iron Age).[3]

In Hildebrand's wide-ranging essay entitled *The Early Iron Age in Norrland* (1869), the typological descriptions are far more numerous and more deliberate in their expression.[4] A careful perusal, however, indicates that the different types which Hildebrand actually placed in a time schedule in this essay were, to a quite predominant extent, dated with the aid of the find contexts. This was done especially by noting analogies with material from the great Danish bog finds (but also with the Sjørup bog find in Scania, for example). In this work, moreover, Hildebrand proclaimed in principle the great chronological importance of the find contexts, including those of the coin finds and the bog finds.[5] In the main, one may describe the chronological method used in this work as an application of the grouping combination method and the grouping type-analogy method, the results of which are presented in a sometimes quite expressive, descriptive typology.

On the whole, the same judgment applies to Montelius' book *The Bronze Age in Northern and Central Sweden*,[6] which he himself regarded as his first typological work. The kinds of object which, according to his own, later statement, he dealt with typologically in this book were 'fibulae, hanging vessels, shaft-hole axes, knives and swords'.[7] It is quite right that one meets with more or less clearly arranged, typological series for these artefact groups.[8] But, at the same time, it is clear, if one takes the trouble to check all the references which fill out the account of the material, that nevertheless Montelius here based the fundamental dating to a large extent on the find contexts.

In order to get a better perspective on the chronological analysis underlying this work, we should remember the general state of archaeological knowledge of Bronze Age chronology at the time when Montelius began his studies of the Bronze Age.

As early as the Copenhagen congress in 1869, Montelius had suggested that the more important types of antiquities should be distributed between an early and a late period of the Bronze Age.[9] He made this distribution quite evidently under the guidance of what was known about Bronze Age burial customs. Without referring directly to Worsaae, he here gives a description of these burial customs which is, in the main, identical with Worsaae's:[10] (a) large, stone coffins containing uncremated corpses, (b) small, stone coffins containing cremated corpses, (c) oak coffins containing uncremated corpses, (d) small coffins containing burnt bones, and (e) funerary urns containing burnt bones.[11] However, in the first part of *The Antiquities of Hallan* (1869b), which was published at the same time, Montelius refers directly to Worsaae on this question, as well as to Boye's investigations of Bronze Age mounds in Halland, which Montelius – unlike Boye himself – found confirmed Worsaae's conclusions.[12] Montelius has testified also in his book *Swedish Antiquities* (1872a) that his chronological starting-point for the Bronze Age was the burial customs.[13]

At the Bologna conference in 1871, Montelius cited Worsaae's grouping of grave types directly as the basis for the chronological division of the Bronze Age. On this occasion, he referred to three different kinds of burial customs: (a) the early Bronze Age graves with coffins containing uncremated bodies, (b) the middle Bronze Age graves with coffins containing cremated bodies, and (c) the late Bronze Age cremation graves containing bone receptacles in the form of small stone coffins or clay vessels. But, he added, 'as for the weapons and the other antiquities found in these graves, the difference

Fig. 34. Hans Hildebrand (1842–1913), Swedish archaeologist, numismatist and historian, in his younger days.

is also very great'.[14] Montelius was indicating that the artefacts could, with the aid of the burial custom, be divided into three chronological groups. It was this further step which Worsaae himself had hesitated to take and which became the fixed starting-point for the thereafter increasingly developed chronology of the Bronze Age.

In this connection, the exhibitions at the museums of archaeology must not be ignored. They represented scientific standpoints to a considerable extent and their role as mediators of facts was even greater before photography became generally accepted in archaeology. The museums of archaeology were just as much a part of the generally available fund of knowledge as the scientific literature.

It is not without interest to note, in the first place, that the importance of keeping the finds together in the public exhibitions seems to have been realized at an early date, both in Copenhagen and in Stockholm. It may be gathered even from Sorterup's catalogue of 1846 of Thomsen's exhibition at Christiansborg that many collective finds were exhibited as units.[15] According to Nils Gustaf Bruzelius, the same principle prevailed in the Stockholm collections recently arranged by Bror Emil Hildebrand in 1847. On this point, Bruzelius reported to Thomsen after his visit there in 1851 that: ' . . . also the Stone and the Bronze Ages were far more abundantly and better represented than I expected. What I particularly liked was that the finds were kept together, which enabled one to determine more easily and with greater certainty the ages of items found individually'.[16]

This early established realization of the scientific importance of the collective find seems to have been passed on when the respective collections were transferred to the new premises in Prindsens Palads in Copenhagen in 1853 and to the new National Museum building in Stockholm in 1865–6. Judging from the first exhibition catalogue for the Museum of National Antiquities, compiled by Montelius in 1872, collective finds seem to have been kept together also in the new arrangements.[17]

When Worsaae took office as Director of the National Museum in 1865, one of his aims was to try, more consistently than before, to have *all* collective finds exhibited as units.[18] This endeavour is also clearly expressed in the different museum catalogues, new editions of which rapidly succeeded each other from this time onwards.

As an example, I may select the 1868 catalogue of the Copenhagen exhibition, written by Engelhardt. It shows the conditions when Montelius was beginning his studies of the Bronze Age. Considerable space on the premises was reserved for collective burial finds and deposits. What was more, the Bronze-Age burial finds were distributed into several different groups, which were, it is true, not directly dated but were nevertheless closely connected with Worsaae's chronology of burial customs. In proper order were exhibited finds from (a) oak coffins containing unburnt bones, (b) stone coffins containing unburnt bones, (c) full-length coffins containing burnt bones, (d) small coffins containing burnt bones, and (e) clay funerary urns containing burnt bones.[19]

It is essential to bear these conditions in mind when reading Hildebrand's and Montelius' early chronological works on the Bronze Age, particularly Hildebrand's *History of the Fibula* and Montelius' *The Bronze Age in Northern and Central Sweden*.[20] The originally stratigraphically demonstrated division of the forms of Bronze Age graves into three chronological groups was at this time a common property of so obvious a nature that it did not require constant explanation and references but could to a large extent be taken for granted.

As early as the end of the 1860s, Montelius had begun his unique and fundamental work by collecting information about all the available Bronze Age finds in Scandinavia and northern Europe. By 1869, he had already listed all the Bronze Age objects, not only in the museums in Stockholm, Lund and Uppsala but also in 30 other public and private collections in Sweden.[21] The find reports in *The Bronze Age* show clearly that Montelius had widened his find survey to comprise the other Scandinavian material and the continental and especially the northern-German material, partly by including the collections and partly by making extensive studies of the literature.[22]

Thus, as early as the beginning of the 1870s, Montelius knew about an enormous material of finds dating from the Bronze Age. The references in *The Bronze Age* show that, to him, this was also current knowledge. Even if we content ourselves with taking into account only the finds named there, it turns out that Montelius had access to closed burial finds and deposits in sufficient numbers to enable him to construct an approximate, chronological framework for the more important artefact groups solely on the basis of the find combinations. The 'typological' investigations in *The Bronze Age* would seem to have originated to a large extent from a find chronology. This 'typology' can be regarded chiefly as a simple, supplementary interpolation between chronological reference points already given by the finds and as an explanatory description of the evolutionary connections which these reference points had revealed.

In this work, Montelius describes one find after another in geographical order. However, he halts at the more important finds and antiquities, in order to place them in a chronological context, with comparisons over the whole of the northern-European region. In this connection, he often sketches the 'typological' evolution of the present form of the object.

Montelius deals with the chronologically important group of fibulae in connection with the description of a deposit from Simtuna in Västmanland, consisting of a spectacle fibula and a disc-headed pin dating from the late Bronze Age. He gives a careful description of the circumstances in which the spectacle fibulae were found within the Scandinavian Bronze Age region and states that he has recorded no less than 66 specimens of the Simtuna form (i.e. period-5 and period-6 types). By way of summary, he declares, as regards the fibula and the pin from Simtuna, that they 'date from the last part of the Bronze Age, as is unanimously shown by the circumstances under which such ornaments have been found on many occasions'.[23]

As regards the long and narrow fibulae characteristic of the early Bronze Age (i.e. the period-2 type), Montelius observes simply that they have long been dated in the early Bronze Age. They certainly were thus dated also by a series of well-known finds in inhumation graves, for example, the Danish Treenhøi find, to which Montelius refers in other connections.[24] It may moreover be worth pointing out that Montelius also had access to Madsen's *Afbildninger*, with its presentation of a series of important closed finds, above all, burial finds.[25] Of the fibulae characteristic of periods 3 and 4, Montelius mentions only finds of the later form (the deposit from Kostraede Banker).[26]

A glance at Montelius' *Dating in the Bronze Age* shows furthermore that practically all the burial finds and deposits containing these forms of fibula which are reported in this work were known at the beginning of the 1870s.[27] Since Montelius sometimes shows a detailed knowledge of the Danish finds in *The Bronze Age* there is reason to suppose that here he must be implying that he has a considerable knowledge of the finds of these fibulae. Even the fact that his fibula forms 3 and 4[28] were known from several finds in graves in the form of small coffins containing burnt bones[29] must have been guidance enough for Montelius to place them in the middle Bronze Age *between* the other forms of fibula.[30] In other words, there seems to have been very little scope for Montelius to arrange the Bronze Age fibulae in chronological order without first having been influenced in important respects by the find contexts. There can have been no question of a pure typology in the true sense (a grading type analogy).

As regards the hanging vessels, Montelius' dependence on the find contexts is even more obvious. He gives references to different closed finds for all his more important types of hanging vessels. The collective witness of these finds cannot have afforded very much elbow-room for independent, typological conclusions.[31]

However, it is quite natural that no one should be able to express a definite opinion about the underlying arguments for the type series which Montelius drew up in this work. His argumentation is throughout too brief for this purpose. As a general rule, it would also seem to be true to say that the further we go into the 1870s, the more difficult it becomes to follow the argumentation in the investigations of the Swedish typologists. Concurrently with the fact that knowledge increased and experience accumulated, more and more facts came to be understood as self-evident.

However, this applies to a far greater extent to Hans Hildebrand, who, with his restless intellect, does not seem to have been attracted to the laborious work of reporting.

Fig. 35. Oscar Montelius, as a middle-aged man.

In his book *The Early Iron Age in Norrland*,[32] he was still reporting with a certain amount of care the grounds of his argumentation as regarded the find contexts. But from *A History of the Fibula* onwards, he worked in this respect for the most part with an implied body of knowledge. The account given in his work on fibulae thereby came to be markedly 'typological' in form. In this work, one finds the genealogical imagery and the evolutionary terminology of the whole of classical typology completely developed, in a way which has few counterparts in nineteenth-century archaeological literature.[33] This is far less marked in Montelius' own work on fibulae, *Bronze-Age Fibulae*, in which moreover he first reports the typological, evolutionary connections and then gives a detailed account of the find circumstances which are to confirm the correctness of the typological series.[34]

The originator of classical typology

From the account given above it will be quite clear that the earliest manifestations of a systematic 'typology' are to be found in the works of Hans Hildebrand and not in those of Oscar Montelius. Hildebrand was accordingly, in practice, the originator of Swedish archaeological typology. However, the question also has a formal aspect.

At the congress held in Bologna in October 1871, Hans Hildebrand gave an address on the Bronze Age fibulae.[35] For the occasion, he had had printed a separate booklet containing illustrations and entitled *Les fibules de l'âge du bronze*, for distribution among the participants in the congress.[36] This booklet illustrates the first really 'typological' series in the development of the Scandinavian Bronze Age fibulae. In this way, it anticipates Montelius' account in *The Bronze Age* in which the section on the fibulae was certainly sent to press during the spring of 1871 but did not appear until the following spring,[37] at approximately the same time as the first few instalments of Hildebrand's *A History of the Fibula*.[38]

Both Hildebrand and Montelius have testified that they observed the typological connection between the Scandinavian forms of fibula independently of each other.[39] But Montelius has also commented on this discovery in words which give the reader to understand that the object of their common discovery was the typological method as such.[40] It is the latter statements which have come to characterize posterity's view of this question.[41]

Hildebrand's comment on the question of the fibula typology is as follows:

> When, during June 1870, I visited the museums in Schwerin and Hanover, I noticed the connection between these fibulae. When I returned home in May 1871, my friend and fellow-worker Dr. Montelius drew my attention to the connection between them, particularly between types A, K and L, which he had discovered in the meantime by his studies in the Swedish and Danish collections only.[42]

Hildebrand is here speaking only of the typological connection between the fibula types and not at all of typology as a method – quite naturally, seeing that, as I mentioned above, he had already in *The Early Iron Age in Norrland* (1869) dealt with artefacts at least as typologically as Montelius did several years later in *The Bronze Age*. That the fibula typology came to be regarded for so long as the first example of typological method is certainly connected with the fact that, when he had to give an account of the early typological literature, Montelius cited *A History of the Fibula* and parts of *The Pre-historic Peoples of Europe*[43] as the only works from Hildebrand's pen.

What Hildebrand really pointed out was that, in his work on the fibulae, he had made the 'first *detailed* attempt to raise the science of the material culture up to the typological stage'.[44] In this, he was quite correct, seeing that, as I mentioned earlier, *A History* is, in respect of typology, far more developed than either his own previous works or Montelius' contemporary work in the typological field.

Although Hans Hildebrand was, above all others, the originator of typology, Montelius nevertheless stands out as the most prominent typologist, less on account of his chronological works than of his contributions to methodological theory. Hildebrand did not specialize deeply in chronological research; the development of a chronological methodology was a far less important question to him than to Montelius. It was instead Montelius who explained in greater detail the typological method of working and propagated this method in both scientific and popular connections. This exegetic work of his has decisively influenced posterity's view of the scientific methods of early archaeology and of Montelius himself as a scientist.

Those of Montelius' writings on the Bronze Age which stand out as the most 'typo-logical' are perhaps the different papers which he presented at international congresses. Like Hans Hildebrand, Montelius took part with zest in the great international con-gresses of archaeologists, which meant so much for the vitality of this young science.[45] On account of the small space which is available in such connections, congress lectures usually take the form of a presentation of a piece of research work, a summary, in which little space is devoted to describing the analysis which underlies the results. This applies in an extraordinarily high degree to Montelius' various contributions,[46] in which he pre-sents the results of his investigations of the Bronze Age chronology to a large extent in the form of a descriptive, explanatory typology. These contributions have helped to a large extent to spread the idea that Montelius was a thoroughgoing typologist, as a research worker in general and as a chronologist of the Bronze Age in particular.

Two terms 'type' and 'typology'
We meet with the actual term 'typology' for the first time in Hans Hildebrand's pamphlet *Prehistoric Archaeology: Its Task, Requirements and Rights*. This was written during the New Year holidays in 1872–3 and appeared in print in the middle of January 1873.[47] Hildebrand presented the term and concept also in the first part of *The Prehis-toric Peoples of Europe*, which appeared at the end of 1873.[48] During the summer and autumn of the same year, he also conducted a course 'with daily lectures on archaeo-logical typology'.[49] Finally, he presented the method as such also in *A History*, most of the parts of which appeared during 1873 and 1874.[50]

We do not meet with the term 'typology' in Montelius' works until a few years later, namely in the two articles *Sur l'âge du bronze en Suède* and *Sur les poignées des épées et des poignards en bronze*[51] included in the printed report of the Stockholm congress. This makes it likely that Montelius used the term at the congress in September 1874 in connection with the first-mentioned lecture, but it is also possible that it was added later when the papers were edited for printing. The paper about the swords, on the other hand, was not presented at the congress; it was written as a supplement to the first one and was published in an appendix to the main report. It seems to have been delivered to the editor at the latest at the turn of the year (1875–6)[52] and at the earliest in July 1875.[53]

Thus, we may declare that it was Hans Hildebrand who introduced the term 'typology' in Scandinavian archaeology.

The Russian archaeologist Gorodzov has stated that the term 'typology' was introduced by the French zoologist de Blainville, who worked at the beginning of the nineteenth century.[54] If this was really the case, the term would nevertheless not seem to have circulated to any appreciable extent in scientific circles during the nineteenth century. It is not very likely that Hildebrand would have studied the work of de Blainville, who, as an investigator of species, was moreover far from sympathizing with any theory of evolution, even one in a pre-Darwinist sense.[55] It is also not very likely that Hildebrand would have derived the term 'typology' from theology, in which it had long been in use, though in a completely different sense. It was not particularly current in theological discussions during the period in question.

It seems most reasonable to assume that Hans Hildebrand independently devised the archaeological term 'typology' by dressing the Swedish word *typlära* (type theory) in the kind of linguistic costume characteristic of the period and that he did this in order to bring to the fore and to give cogency to the new methodological endeavours in archaeology which were initiated at the beginning of the 1870s. Consequently with the increased concentration on detailed datings, greater demands were made on the type classification. Type analysis and type-grouping now became more essential operations than they had been before. The newly gained knowledge that developmental connections could be traced between artefact types may very well have aroused in Hildebrand's mind the association with the biological theory of species, which was highly topical in Sweden at this period, and given him the idea of *the term* 'typology'. In the two written contexts in which Hildebrand first presented 'typology', we in fact also find an – admittedly general – comparison between typology and the biological theory of species.[56]

Although the concept of 'type' was an old one in archaeology, other terms and expressions were used during the beginning and the middle of the nineteenth century. The word 'form' was often used. This was also the term which Montelius used in his first archaeological work, for example, *From the Iron Age* (1869).[57] In print, he seems to have begun to use the term 'type' in 1872 but rarely; he usually preferred the word 'form'.[58] It was not until the latter part of the 1870s that Montelius came to use more consistently the terms 'type' and 'typology'.

Hans Hildebrand, on the other hand, consistently used the term 'type' even in his first scientific works, i.e. from 1866 onwards;[59] as far as I can see, he was the first to do so in Scandinavian archaeology. In his correspondence, he used the term 'type' as early as 1862.[60] It is noteworthy that his father Bror Emil Hildebrand also did so, on one of the few occasions when he briefly discussed the forms of archaeological artefacts in his later works, namely in his famous essay on the dating of the rock-carvings (1869).[61]

Typology and numismatics

There is also a field of research which closely connects Bror Emil and Hans Hildebrand with the term 'type'. This field is numismatics. There immediately presents itself the idea of connecting Hans Hildebrand's very early and thorough, numismatic training with his natural way of using the term 'type' even at the beginning of his archaeological research. When he was still a boy, Hans was introduced to numismatics by his father.[62] In both the editions of his doctoral thesis, Hans appears as a pioneering archaeological and historical interpreter of the finds of Iron Age coins.[63] He also appears at an early age as an independent numismatist. In his essay entitled *The Fölhagen Find* (1870), for example, he deals with a large, numismatic material of over 400, mainly German coins.[64]

This is not an unimportant point, for in numismatics 'type' had long been a term in general use.[65] Not least Bror Emil Hildebrand himself preferred to use this term, especially in *Anglo-Saxon Coins* (1846) but also in earlier works. While Hildebrand Senior touched in his research to a very small extent upon such analysis of archaeological artefacts as might give him occasion to use the term 'type' in archaeological contexts,[66] this was the more natural to his son. Hildebrand Junior was one of the few scientists who, during this important period in the history of archaeology, was in direct contact with both numismatics and archaeology. As a numismatist, he inherited directly his father's knowledge and it must have been wholly natural to him to make use of the term 'type' in archaeological connections. In these circumstances, his natural way of using the term 'type' from the very beginning does not appear as anything unexpectedly new but as a natural tradition.

However, the important thing in this connection is that, in numismatics, especially as it appears in Bror Emil Hildebrand's *Anglo-Saxon Coins*, we meet with formulations and turns of expression which we have generally come to regard as belonging to the subject of archaeological typology. This does not happen exceptionally but often recurs.

In the first place, the classification in *Anglo-Saxon Coins* is made consistently in types. These types are named alphabetically, i.e. type A, B, C, D, E, etc., and are often provided with subsidiary numbers[67] in the way which was later adopted in archaeology, especially by Hans Hildebrand.[68] A few quotations will best illustrate this numismatic 'typology' in the works of Bror Emil Hildebrand: 'Type C1, for which patterns will be found in . . . Type C2, which is only a later reconstruction of C1 . . . Type B2 differs . . . from type B1 and forms a . . . transitional form to type C . . . Type C has been copied from Aethelred's type E . . . Type D has evidently been formed from Aethelred's type F and its variant, type F*a* . . . Type F constitutes a kind of transitional form between Edward's early and late types . . . Type G begins a new series.'[69]

The fact that archaeological grading typology emanated in the first place from Hans Hildebrand allows us to surmise that we have to seek in numismatics – especially in Bror Emil Hildebrand's presentation of it – for one of the elements from which typology was formed step by step.

There is a natural explanation for the fact that, in numismatics, scholars so early made use of detailed classification systems of an almost biological kind and that they formulated and described the developmental connections long before this became common in prehistoric archaeology. The numismatists were, in the main, free from the enormous dating problems with which the research workers in prehistory wrestled so long. In most cases, the classification of the coins into main chronological groups was a self-evident operation, owing to the historical evidence given by the coins themselves. Questions of dating therefore came to be chiefly concerned with the fine classification. Consequently, numismatics had a fairly well-constructed, chronological framework to start with, long before prehistoric archaeology, with the aid of the find contexts, had reached the favourable position in which a descriptive typology naturally appears. Thus, numismatists became aware at an early stage that historically dated coin types or coin groups which were close to each other in time also resembled each other and that they did not succeed each other abruptly without the subsequent type bearing traces of the preceding type.

The form of descriptive typology which occurs, for example, in Bror Emil Hildebrand's *Anglo-Saxon Coins* (1846) should therefore not be regarded as a surprisingly early example of the typological way of looking at things, which one has necessarily to try to trace back to some special, ideological background. It is, on the contrary, natural to find, in connection with a factual material of that kind, that it offers a detailed chronology constructed by non-archaeological means. Nor is it surprising to find the next step – a more independent typology – in an investigation of a coin material with unusually well-established, fixed points in history. I am thinking of John Evans' book *The Coins of the Ancient Britons* (1864),[70] which has often been pointed out as one of the earliest eixamples of conscious typological method. On the other hand, Evans did not transfer this 'typological' way of looking things to his later, major work on prehistory, *The Ancient Bronze Implements* (1872), in which he discusses a material with fairly few chronological points of reference in the finds. The consistent use of the term 'type' in this work and the system of classification, using figures, is, however, symptomatic of the numismatically trained archaeologist in prehistory.[71]

From a different point of departure, Almgren has drawn attention to the share which Bror Emil Hildebrand in particular may have had in the origin of typology, namely that, together with Hans Hildebrand and Oscar Montelius, he may have realized the developmental relation between the artefacts in connection with the practical exhibition work involved in the re-arrangement of the Stockholm collections in 1865–6.[72] To all appearances, Bror Emil Hildebrand alone seems to have arranged both the Stone Age and the Bronze Age exhibitions, while Hans Hildebrand and Montelius helped with the Iron Age exhibition.[73] However, judging from the different exhibition catalogues dating from the 1870s, we would not seem to have to reckon that there was any strictly typological ordering of the Stone Age and Bronze Age collections.[74] At the end of the 1870s, the Bronze Age still seems to have been divided up into only two periods.[75] Even as late as 1880, when Hans Hildebrand succeeded his father as Chief Custodian of National Antiquities and head of the Museum, he expressed doubts about the correctness of dividing the Bronze Age artefacts even into two different periods.[76] To all appearances, the Bronze Age exhibition was not given a more detailed chronological order until after Montelius had published his *Dating in the Bronze Age*.

As far as the Iron Age is concerned, a clearer connection is to be seen between the exhibition work and the typology. It was precisely within this period that Hans Hildebrand operated in his first works, in which he describes the developmental connections in typological terms. He states that, in connection with his work on his doctoral thesis, he had to independently arrange the Iron Age finds on the Swedish mainland and Gotland;[77] it was, of course, particularly to the forms of the Gotland ornaments that he devoted his first typological studies. Thus, it seems possible that the practical exhibition work may be counted as one of the elements which have to be taken into account in forming an opinion about the origin of typology.

Typology and Darwinism

'Typology is the application of Darwinism to the products of human labour' is the introductory sentence in Nils Åberg's famous definition of typology in 1929, in which he pushes the analogy between the evolution of the artefacts and that of organic life to its extreme limit.[78] Åberg's views constitute a sharpening of Montelius' typological theory, from which they undoubtedly emanate.

It was also Montelius' methodological theory that mediated the idea that the origin of typology was directly connected with Darwinism, in spite of the fact that Hans Hildebrand put forward the analogy 11 years before Montelius first made a clear allusion to the theory of evolution and 25 years before he used the word 'Darwinism' in print in connection with typology. In fact, Montelius does not seem to have mentioned Darwinism by name on more than one occasion and that was not until the end of the century.[79]

In Hans Hildebrand's pamphlet, *Scientific Archaeology* (1873), however, we find the first analogy between typology and the theory of biological evolution. At the same time, this is, as far as I can discover, the only time that Hildebrand directly apostrophizes Darwin. The portions concerned read as follows:

> One might call the new stage which archaeology has entered 'the typological stage'. Our next task is to establish *the types*, to ascertain which of them are characteristic of each region, to search out the type's affinities, and to unfold their history; and the type to be investigated in this sense is both the finished instrument and the smallest ornament which adorns it . . . The many similar objects are only ostensibly duplicates, the many axes . . . do not have the same importance as the same number of specimens of an animal species in the zoological museum. Slight differences appear in these axe specimens, and thus they do not in general correspond to specimens of animals but to species and varieties; here, the formation of varieties is greater on account of man's influence on developments . . . Under the influence of two factors – the practical need and the craftsman's taste – a great many forms arise, each of which has to struggle for its existence; one does not find what it needs for its existence and succumbs, but the other moves forward and produces a whole series of forms. If any science at present needs its Darwin, it is comparative archaeology, and the more abundant the slight differences are, the more deeply one feels in this sphere the absence of the missing intermediate links.[80]

In the same year, 1873, Hans Hildebrand expressed the comparison in *The Prehistoric*

Peoples as follows:

> The stations during this development are the types, which correspond to the species in the organic world, though not the species as they are now, bilaterally ordered, but as they occur in palaeontology, chronologically ordered. However, there is a difference in relation to the palaeontological series in that in the culture-historical series one can more clearly distinguish the rise, the culmination and the fall. From this, it is also clear that the types of cultural objects cannot be so sharply divided as the species in nature at the present day; one finds transitional forms in large numbers, but one gradually learns to distinguish certain forms which have become constant, while others show an uncertain fluctuation.[81]

The first time that Montelius alluded to the biological theory of evolution was in *The Methods and Materials* (1884), from which the following quotation has been taken:

> The methodology of prehistoric archaeology has long been like that of natural science. Like the latter, the former has also now entered a new stage.
>
> The natural scientist is no longer content to describe the different species and to study their lives. He tries to find out the internal connection that binds them together and to show how one species has developed from the other.
>
> What the species is to the natural scientist, the type is to the archaeologist. The productions of nature which resemble each other in all essentials and which have a common origin are considered to belong to the same species. When it is a question of the productions of human labour, the same definition can be used of the type.
>
> The prehistoric archaeologist no longer regards it as his only task to describe and compare the antiquities from different countries and to investigate life in these countries in bygone days. He now tries to trace the internal connection between the types and to show how one has developed from the other. We call this *typology*.
>
> Before one has become familiar with the history of human culture, one is apt to consider individual freedom as so great that the types in the world of human labour cannot play the same part as the species play in the world of nature. However, one soon finds that they really do so and that the types of human works, like the animal and plant species, obey laws in their evolution.[82]
>
> . . . it is only recently, through the typological method, that the archaeologist has learned not only to distinguish correctly one type from another but also to *follow the development of the types from each other*, in the same way as the natural scientist now not only distinguishes the species but also tries to find their internal connections.
>
> The reason for this view, which differs from that of the Swedish archaeologists . . . lies, in my opinion, to no small extent in the fact that the former, before they began to work as archaeologists, made themselves more or less familiar with the methods of the natural scientists. It is natural that the scientist who does not know this method in advance . . . will have more difficulty in understanding what we

mean by a method which, in actual fact, is nothing else than that of the natural scientist, although it is applied not to the productions of nature but to relics of man's prehistory.[83]

The second example is from the article entitled *Typology or the Theory of Evolution Applied to Human Labour* (1899)[84] which has, more than any other, set its stamp on posterity's view of the typological method. Even the title indicates that Montelius is now presenting the simile in a more categorical fashion:

> What the species is to the natural scientist, the type is to the prehistoric archaeologist, and the latter . . . no longer regards it as his only task to describe and compare the antiquities from different countries and to investigate life in these countries in bygone days. He now tries to trace the internal connection which exists between the types and to show how one type, like one species, has developed from the other. We call this *typology*.[85]
>
> In a typological investigation – as in the corresponding investigations of the natural scientist – the 'rudimentary formations' deserve special attention.[86]
>
> That I wish to speak at a conference of natural scientists about the typological method is not, however, due so much to the great importance of this method to the archaeologist as to the possibility that it may be of interest to the natural scientist to see, on the one hand, how we use, generally speaking, the same method as he does – in that we collect as large a material as possible and arrange it so that the results are immediately obvious – and, on the other, how we stand, in respect of the theory of evolution, on a purely Darwinistic ground. That, as regards the productions of nature, it is possible to follow the evolution of one form or one species from the other has, of course, as we are all aware, long been known. But it is only recently that we have discovered, in the way that I have just shown, that a quite similar development can actually also be shown as regards the productions of human labour. This should interest the natural scientist so much the more as man is, of course, in himself, regarded as a production of nature, also an object of his studies.
>
> In actual fact, it is also an extremely wonderful thing that man should in his work be subject to an evolution governed by laws. Is human freedom so restricted that we could not freely make whatever forms we wished? Are we compelled to go, step by step, from one form to another that is only slightly different?
>
> Before one has investigated the matter more closely, one would certainly be tempted to reply 'No' to these questions. But when one has become, by a thorough study, familiar with the remarkable phenomena of which I have just spoken, one finds that the answer must be 'Yes'. Evolution may proceed more quickly or more slowly, but man is always compelled, in his creation of new forms, to follow the law of evolution, as it applies to the rest of nature.[87]

The analogy presented in these quotations between the evolution of organic life and that of the cultural products is certainly basically false.[88] But even an analogy like this may be of importance in providing a stimulus, and this analogy undoubtedly influenced subsequent research. However, the comparison is defective not only in principle but also in details, a few of which will be touched upon below.

The analogy between the concept of species and the concept of type was not a happy one, at any rate not as Montelius formulated it. The evolutionary concept of species has and had a much wider content than the concept of type in archaeology. As the term 'type' is used, it corresponds primarily to 'variety' in biology, while the concept of species would rather correspond to the concept of artefact category, group or the like ('oval brooches', 'socketed axe', 'microliths', etc.).

Nor is the agreement with the theory of descent particularly striking. This starts from the assumption that all organic life originates from only one or a few primitive cells or primitive types. This is by no means the case in the 'typological' sphere. There, one has instead to reckon with a large number of separate lines of development, which emanate from many different, primitive types. The lines of descent in typology are also in many cases short and are characterized by a most un-Darwinian and frequent production of original types.

As is evident, Montelius – unlike Hildebrand – never referred to the theory of natural selection, the actual explanatory theory in Darwinism. Without this theory, i.e. the theory of 'the struggle for existence', which gives rise to the natural selection which is the real driving force in evolution, little remains of the special character of Darwinism. Montelius' analogy with the theory of evolution thereby appears even more vague and general.

If we should attempt at all to place archaeological typology in any biological theory of evolution, the preceding remarks will show that Darwinism is not the most likely one. In that case, a pre-Darwinian theory of evolution might rather come into question.

Fig. 36. Hans Hildebrand in his study.

One's mind goes primarily to the concepts belonging to the romantic biology of the early nineteenth century, with its idea of parallel development and its notions about a gradual creation of new forms.[89]

If we are really to interpret Hildebrand's and Montelius' analogies with Darwinism as seriously intended from the methodological point of view, we must accordingly observe that they testify to ignorance not only of the process underlying cultural and historical evolution but also of biological evolution, as it appears in Darwinism. But it would undoubtedly appear to be more reasonable to interpret this analogy more as an illustrative simile, a loose imagery with no profound methodological purpose. It would be an under-estimate to imagine that Hildebrand and Montelius were not aware that their comparisons between typology and the theory of evolution would not bear a critical, scientific examination. This idea seems to be particularly unreasonable as regards Hans Hildebrand. All his writings on cultural history breathe the most profound understanding of the creative forces which underlie the development and shaping of the purely historical material. This is especially true of *The Prehistoric Peoples* with its analogy with the theory of evolution just quoted above. It is difficult to imagine any scope for misunderstanding on Hildebrand's part on this point, especially as he had had an unusually wide training in the field of natural history. When Hildebrand speaks in the above-mentioned work of an organic connection between the types, he moreover emphasizes at the same time that the type is a 'manifestation of something human'.[90] Speaking of the possibility of drawing up typological pedigrees, he points out in *A History* that 'in doing so, I forget that the things which I have in front of me are dead. In them, life really also reveals itself, although this life is not theirs, but that of the peoples to whose culture they belong, whose products they are, to whose character they bear witness'.[91] A little further on, Hildebrand speaks directly of the nature of the actual process of evolution:

> By a kind of composing activity, One inserts new motifs below this transitional type, and thus quite new types of a decidedly developed kind emerge . . . When it is a question of something so simple as making a fibula, the expression 'composing activity' may well seem somewhat exaggerated, but the human mind is one and the same in its activity and this is expressed in repeated analogies in the most varying fields of activity. This genesis of new types from the old by the insertion of new motifs is dependent on the same process of evolution as we perceive in higher regions, as, for example, when, in the realm of mythology, new ideas are infused into a divine figure created by the popular consciousness, after which the god appears to have been refined and transported to a higher sphere of life.[92]

In another connection, Hildebrand speaks of 'the agreement between types which is due to a continuous development in the creative human spirit'.[93]

It is justifiable to point out that *neither Hildebrand nor Montelius suggested on any occasion that Darwinism or the theory of evolution gave them the actual idea of typology.* On this point, posterity has been inclined to read a deeper meaning into their statements than these statements actually express.

Commentators have often pointed to Montelius' specialization in natural science during his student years, in order to explain his interest in the theory of evolution.[94] But, in doing so, they disregard the fact that a certain amount of basic training in natural science was still common at that period in a university degree specializing in the humanities. It turns out that even Hans Hildebrand, who is often regarded as a typical humanist, had, in actual fact, wide interests in the sphere of natural science; botany, geology, mineralogy, mathematics and astronomy were some of the subjects in which he received instruction at the university, alongside the humanities.[95] He early became a member of both the sections of the Natural Science Society (the Section for Chemistry and Mineralogy and the Section for Botany and Zoology).[96] He gave at least two lectures in the latter section, one of which was purely botanical.[97]

Hildebrand's interest in natural science is expressed time after time in his scholarly works, in distinct contrast to Montelius' research, which has very little connection with natural science. Hildebrand was particularly interested in geology and palaeontology, subjects which were important for the investigation of the palaeolithic Stone Age, which was highly topical in western Europe around 1860 and later. In August 1862, Hildebrand and Gustaf Retzius, the anthropologist, were invited to visit Henry Christy, the English banker and collector of ethnographic items, in London. Christy had been fascinated by the abundant cave finds in France and had initiated, as a patron and colleague, direct collaboration with Eduard Lartet. During this visit, Hildebrand gained a good insight into the new, palaeolithic finds in both England and France and borrowed from Christy all his literature on the subject.[98] Probably Hildebrand had already got to know about the existence of the Abbeville finds when he visited Paris with his father the year before (1861) and in this connection also met Christy, who had paid his expenses.[99] Six months after his return from England, Hildebrand gave a lecture on, inter alia, the Abbeville finds to the Society of Natural Science Students in Uppsala.[100] He had probably heard during his stay in London about Charles Lyell's book *The Antiquity of Man*, which had not then been published.[101] Hildebrand mentioned it expectantly during the autumn and bought it at once when it was published in the spring of 1863.[102]

In Lyell's book, a whole chapter is devoted to accounts of Darwin's new theories,[103] which Hildebrand must have heard discussed during his visit to London. On one occasion in 1865, he privately defended Darwin but he was then still not acquainted with Darwin's own works.[104] However, their visit to England seems to have aroused, once and for all, both his and Retzius' interest[105] in the earliest history of human culture.

Hildebrand's wide interests in the sciences that deal with ancient times was expressed in reviews, articles[106] and books. They appear particularly clearly in his great work *The Prehistoric Peoples of Europe* a work which, in its broad scope, has no contemporary counterparts anywhere. Hildebrand demonstrates, in various sections of this book, an impressive knowledge of the modern points of view in anthropology, palaeontology, geology and palaeolithic prehistory in general.[107] He is well informed about the more or less Darwinistic research into the earliest history and cultural history of man, a literature which he also to a considerable extent added to his personal library.[108] He seems to have been acquainted at least with Darwin's *The Descent of Man*.[109] As far as Montelius is concerned, on the other hand, references to Darwinistic literature are practically entirely absent in his works, and this literature is also conspicuous by its absence in the enormous library which he left behind at his death.[110]

It was not until about 1870 that serious attention was paid to Darwinism in public discussions in Sweden. The Swedish edition of *The Origin of Species* appeared in 1871 and that of *The Descent of Man* in the following year.[111] Darwinism was discussed and presented abruptly in a number of different contexts.[112] During the years around and after 1870, the theory of evolution was a burning question in Sweden. The theory of descent had, on the whole, been generally accepted, both internationally and in Sweden, in natural science, although there was increased resistance in some quarters to the actual theory of natural selection.[113]

It is obvious that Hildebrand, like Montelius, was, in a general sense, a Darwinist. However, one does not perceive in either of them any deep commitment to the explanatory theory of Darwinism, and it is possible that they were mainly influenced by Darwinism indirectly, through the general cultural discussions. Hildebrand's and Montelius' Darwinism would seem mainly to have amounted only to their being convinced believers in the idea of evolution and the theory of evolution in quite general terms. One must, of course, expect that the theory of evolution formed an integral part of their overall view of cultural history. But it is a long step from this to the conclusion that Darwinism played a decisive part as the actual impulse which resulted in the establishment of typology *as a method of dating*. On the other hand, it is likely, as I mentioned above, that Hildebrand formulated the actual term 'typology' by analogy with the theory of biological evolution, which was particularly topical just at the beginning of the 1870s, when Hildebrand was trying to define exactly the overall view of chronological method which had previously, step by step, developed on a mainly empirical basis.

Montelius took no active part in the formulation of the 'typological' method. His allusions to Darwinism are few, late and unclear. He did not, any more than Hildebrand, assert that Darwinism had stimulated the genesis of typology. He did not put forward until very much later the analogy with the biological theory of evolution, at a time when this theory had become a fully accepted framework of social reference. There are strong reasons for thinking that we should regard Montelius' comparison with Darwinism only as a way of illustrating, justifying and giving cogency to an archaeological method, a way which, at least originally, was never meant to be taken literally.

The typological language
From about 1870 onwards, the chronological frameworks became denser and form an increasingly complicated pattern that is difficult to survey. There is a greater tendency to present chronological conclusions by describing the results in developmental terms, with no direct account of the grounds for them, a procedure which has here been called 'descriptive typology'. From the 1870s onwards, it becomes more and more difficult to draw clear borderlines between find-combination reasoning, descriptive typology and pure grading typology.

Descriptive, explanatory typology seems to have sprung in a natural way out of observations of the find contexts; as the archaeologists by this means succeeded in chronologically subdividing the material, there arose precisely the possibility of *observing* the connections in the variability and thus also of describing this connection in evolutionary terms.

Descriptive typology is therefore not a definitely time-dependent phenomenon in origin. It appeared when the prerequisite conditions existed, which was naturally at different times for different materials: in the middle of the 1840s in Bror Emil Hildebrand's coin classification, in 1859 in Worsaae's classification of Bronze Age burial customs, during the second half of the 1860s in Hans Hildebrand's Iron Age studies, and at the beginning of the 1870s in Montelius' Bronze Age works and in Vedel's studies of the pre-Roman Iron Age. It is difficult to discern any connection between the first appearance of descriptive typology and evolutionary ideas of either a Darwinian or a pre-Darwinian character.

The step from the explanatory and descriptive to the actively chronological typology (the grading analogy method) would not seem to have been a long one. Concurrently with the fact that the find circumstances increasingly often demonstrated the connection in the culture sequence, archaeologists naturally became aware of the possibility of establishing a relative chronology by going in the opposite direction – by arranging the artefacts in a continuous, chronological order according to the degree of similarity. In the work of both Hans Hildebrand and Oscar Montelius, the two prominent figures in typology, one can clearly observe how explanatory typology passes almost imperceptibly over into chronologically active, evolutionary typology.

When the archaeologists had to describe typological connections, whether descriptive or actively grading, they did so, linguistically, by consistently allowing the artefact material to appear as the subject instead of the object. The correct procedure would, of course, have been to represent the makers, the ancient craftsmen, as the active force behind the changes. But to repeat, in practically every sentence, that the changes took place in the minds of those who made the artefacts was bound to result in a, to say the least, unpalatable dish. In this way, it became natural to design the description as if the mechanism of the change lay instead in the dead material.

It is in this simple fact that I believe that we may seek much of the magic of descriptive typology and its ability to hinder insight into the chains of deduction. Here, we already have the germ of the future analogy with the theory of evolution and of the evolutionary terminology of typology, on the whole. The power which figurative representation has over thought would also seem to bear a considerable proportion of the responsibility for the unrealistic way especially in which the post-Montelian typologists regarded the products of prehistoric culture.

NOTES

1 Arne 1934, pp. 318f.; cf. B. Hildebrand 1943, pp. 104f. and 111, N. Åberg 1943, pp. xiii f., and B. Almgren 1959, pp. 114f. and 119f.
2 B. Almgren 1959, p. 119; cf. N. Åberg 1943, pp. xiii ff.
3 H. Hildebrand 1866, pp. 15ff.
4 H. Hildebrand 1869a, for example, p. 229 (footnote), 267 (footnote), 268, 291f., 294f., 311 and 313.
5 H. Hildebrand 1869a, pp. 225f., 251 and 295.

6 Montelius 1872–3.
7 Montelius 1885a, p. 8. The emphatically typological illustration of the sequence of axes in the printed lecture given at the Bologna congress in 1871 was, to all appearances, first added in connection with the publication (Montelius 1873a, figs. 7–11).
8 Montelius, 1872–3, pp. 219ff., 275ff., 314ff., 331ff., 344ff. and 352ff.
9 Montelius 1875, pp. 253f.
10 Worsaae 1860a.
11 Montelius 1875, pp. 250f.
12 Montelius 1869b, p. 57; cf. 1872c, pp. 198ff.
13 Montelius 1872a, p. 24.
14 Montelius 1873a, p. 288.
15 Sorterup 1846.
16 Letter from N. G. Bruzelius to C. J. Thomsen in December 1851. Archives of the National Museum in Copenhagen.
17 Montelius 1872b.
18 Hindenburg 1869, pp. 388f.; Worsaae 1877, p. 6.
19 Engelhardt 1868, pp. 12ff.
20 H. Hildebrand 1872–80; Montelius 1872–3.
21 Montelius 1875, pp. 249f.
22 Cf. Salin 1922, pp. 11f.; H. Hildebrand 1872–80, pp. 40f., note 1.
23 Montelius 1872–3, pp. 217ff.
24 Montelius 1872–3, pp. 266 and 338.
25 Madsen 1872 and 1876. The latter work seems to have appeared in parts containing plates, long before the year of final printing, since Montelius frequently refers also to part 2.
26 Montelius 1872–3, p. 220.
27 Montelius 1885a, pp. 201–38, 271–307 and pls. 2–5.
28 Montelius 1872–3, p. 220 (corresponding primarily to types VIIC–E in *Dating in the Bronze Age*).
29 Montelius 1885a, pp. 281–8.
30 It will be observed that, in *Nordic Antiquities* (18549), Worsaae reproduced the more important forms of fibula in the right order, though without commenting on the time sequence (Worsaae 1859, pl. 51).
31 Montelius 1872–3, pp. 272ff.
32 H. Hildebrand 1869a.
33 H. Hildebrand 1872–80.
34 Montelius 1880–2.
35 H. Hildebrand 1873c.
36 H. Hildebrand 1871a. He reported from Bologna that 'the 95 copies of the figures which I had with me went like hot cakes'. Letter from Hans Hildebrand to Bror Emil Hildebrand from Bologna, dated 10 October 1871 (in the possession of Professor Karl-Gustaf Hildebrand, Uppsala).
37 Montelius 1872–3. Concerning its publication, see *Antiqvarisk Tidskrift för Sverige* 3 (the back of the second number), *Månadsblad* 2, 1872, February, p. 31, *Månadsblad* 5, 1872, May, p. 79, and Montelius 1872–3, p. 408.
38 H. Hildebrand 1872–80. Concerning its publication, see *Månadsblad* 3, 1872, March, p. 46, *Månadsblad* 6, 1872, June, p. 95, *Månadsblad* 7, 1872, July, p. 110, and Montelius 1880–2, p. 1.
39 H. Hildebrand 1872–80, note on pp. 40f.; Montelius 1878, pp. 9f., and 1885a, p. 8.
40 Montelius 1880–2, p. 3, note 1, and 1884a, p. 2, note 1.
41 For example, Kock 1917, p. 279, Arne 1908, p. 216, and 1922, pp. 8f., Nerman 1921, p. 290, Kossinna 1922, p. 313.
42 H. Hildebrand 1872–80, note on pp. 40f.
43 Montelius 1880–2, p. 3, note 1, and 1884a, p. 2, note 1.
44 H. Hildebrand 1873–80, p. 54, note 1.

45 For example, the congresses in Copenhagen (1869), Bologna (1871), Stockholm (1874) and Budapest (1876). Hans Hildebrand also took part in the Brussels congress in 1872.
46 Montelius 1875, 1873a, 1876a, 1876b and 1877a. Cf. 1874b (the meeting of Scandinavian natural scientists in Copenhagen in 1873). These writings are only reproductions of lectures on Bronze-Age subjects.
47 H. Hildebrand 1873a, p. 16.
48 H. Hildebrand 1873–80, p. 54.
49 *Månadsblad* 23, 1873, November, p. 176; cf. *Månadsblad* 18, 1873, June, pp. 87ff.
50 H. Hildebrand 1872–80, pp. 18f. and 26ff.
51 Montelius 1876a, p. 504 and 1876b, p. 920.
52 Hildebrand refers to the article, occasionally word for word, including the formulation which includes the term 'typology', in an article in *Månadsblad* (1874), which was sent to press on 17 January 1876 (H. Hildebrand 1976a, pp. 125f.).
53 Letter from Oscar Montelius to Hans Hildebrand dated 8 July 1875. ATA.
54 Gorodzov 1933, p. 95. Gorodzov writes, without further explanation, that 'the term "typological method" was introduced into science in Blenwell in 1816'. In all probability, this name 'Blenwell' was the result of a phonetic transcription of the French name 'Blainville' into the Russian alphabet and then a likewise phonetic transcription from Russian into English, made by a translator who was unacquainted with the original French name. Here, Gorodzov is probably referring to Ducrotay de Blainville's book *Prodrome d'une nouvelle distribution du règne animal* (Blainville 1816). Blainville, who was originally a pupil of Cuvier, introduced the term 'type' for Cuvier's four main groups of zoological species (von Holfsten 1922, pp. 395f. and 402).
55 von Hofsten 1928, pp. 39f.
56 Hildebrand 1873a, pp. 16f., and 1873–80, p. 54.
57 Montelius 1869a.
58 Montelius 1872a and 1872–3.
59 H. Hildebrand 1866 and 1869a.
60 Letter from Hans Hildebrand to Bror Emil Hildebrand dated 26 October 1862 (in the possession of Professor Karl-Gustaf Hildebrand, Uppsala).
61 B. E. Hildebrand 1869, pp. 9f.
62 Thordeman 1934, p. 330; Bachman 1969, p. 173, note 89.
63 H. Hildebrand 1866, pp. 18ff. and 61ff., and 1872a, pp. 29ff.
64 H. Hildebrand 1870, pp. 58ff.
65 For example, Brenner 1731, Hallenberg 1800, Schröder 1849, Thomsen 1931–4.
66 B. E. Hildebrand 1846 and 1829.
67 B. E. Hildebrand 1846, pp. 13–300, tables 1–10; cf. 1829, pp. 24–44.
68 H. Hildebrand 1869a, p. 233, 1872–80, for example, pp. 38, 80 and 183f., 1873b, pp. 28ff. and 36ff. Cf. the numismatist Thomsen's letter classification of the gold bracteates (1855, p. 279), which was later taken up and carried on by Montelius (1869a, at the foot of the last page (unnumbered)).
69 B. E. Hildebrand 1846, pp. 5, 13, 144 and 276.
70 Evans 1864, pp. 24ff. and 33ff.
71 Evans 1872.
72 B. Almgren 1959, pp. 115ff.
73 Letter from Hans Hildebrand to an unnamed Danish friend in Copenhagen dated 22 May 1866 (in the possession of Professor Karl-Gustaf Hildebrand, Uppsala).
74 For example, Montelius 1872b and subsequent editions.
75 See, for example, H. Hildebrand 1881, p. 17.
76 H. Hildebrand 1873–80, p. 667 (printed in 1880).
77 H. Hildebrand 1884, p. 124.
78 N. Åberg 1929, section 3.
79 Montelius 1899.

80 H. Hildebrand 1873a, pp. 16f.
81 H. Hildebrand 1873–80, p. 54 (printed in 1873).
82 Montelius 1884a, pp. 1f.
83 Montelius 1884a, p. 27.
84 Montelius 1899. According to Montelius, the article 'agrees in the main with' a lecture which he 'gave at the 15th Congress of Scandinavian Natural Scientists in Stockholm on 12 July 1898' (p. 237, note 1).
85 Montelius 1899, p. 237.
86 Montelius 1899, p. 264; cf. the formulation which recurs word for word in *Die typologische Methode*, 1903, p. 17.
87 Montelius 1899, pp. 267f.; cf. 1903, p. 20.
88 Cf. Johannsen 1917, pp. 90ff., and Nordman 1915.
89 Eriksson 1969, pp. 100ff.
90 H. Hildebrand 1872–80, p. 18.
91 H. Hildebrand 1872–80, p. 27.
92 H. Hildebrand 1872–80, p. 39.
93 H. Hildebrand 1873–80, p. 57.
94 Sernander 1922, p. 52.
95 Montelius took mathematics as a subsidiary subject in his degree in 1868 but had received instruction also in botany and chemistry. Cf. A. Åberg 1966, p. 114, Rydh 1937, p. 34, Lewenhaupt 1922, p. 4, and O. Almgren 1921, pp. 303ff.
96 Letters from H. Hildebrand to B. E. Hildebrand from Uppsala, dated 28 September 1860 and 2 December 1860 (in the possession of Professor Karl-Gustaf Hildebrand, Uppsala).
97 This lecture was given on 1 March 1861 and was entitled *Mortality in the Plant World*. Letter from H. Hildebrand to B. E. Hildebrand, dated 13 March 1861 (in the possession of Professor Karl-Gustaf Hildebrand, Uppsala).
98 Letter from H. Hildebrand to B. E. Hildebrand from London, dated 4 August 1862 (in the possession of Professor Karl-Gustaf Hildebrand, Uppsala).
99 B. Hildebrand 1943, pp. 100ff. See also note 108.
100 The lecture was entitled *The Abbeville Finds, the Kitchen Middens and the Stone-Age Lake-Dwellings* and was given on 19 February 1863. Letters from H. Hildebrand to B. E. Hildebrand from Uppsala, dated 17 and 19 February 1863 (in the possession of Professor Karl-Gustaf Hildebrand, Uppsala University Library, U 1832b); cf. Torstendahl 1964, p. 325.
101 Lyell 1863 (published on 6 February 1863).
102 Letters from H. Hildebrand to B. E. Hildebrand from Uppsala, dated 26 October 1862 and 19 April 1863. Lyell's book was included in the library which Hans Hildebrand left on his death and bears the wording 'Uppsala, 5 April 1863, Hans Hildebrand'. This library is preserved at the Royal Academy of Letters, History and Antiquities in Stockholm.
103 Lyell 1863, pp. 407–23.
104 Torstendahl 1964, p. 326, note 8. See the letter from H. Hildebrand to Elin Hildebrand dated 23 May 1865 (in the possession of Professor Karl-Gustaf Hildebrand, Uppsala).
105 Retzius 1933, pp. 175ff., and 1948, p. 20.
106 H. Hildebrand 1867, 1869b, 1869c and 1882.
107 H. Hildebrand 1873–80 (chapter 1 appeared in 1873 and chapter 2 in 1875–6).
108 Lyell 1863, 1867–8 and 1871, Darwin 1868, Haeckel 1868 and 1873, Huxley 1873, Quatrefages 1870 and Retzius 1873.
109 Darwin 1871b; see H. Hildebrand 1873–80, p. 4, note 1, and p. 14.
110 Lundqvist 1843.
111 Darwin 1871a and 1872.
112 For example, Andersson 1869 and 1871, Quennerstedt 1871 and *Samtiden* 1871. Hildebrand and Montelius themselves contributed to the same journals, in which Darwinism was discussed: H. Hildebrand 1871b (Svensk Tidskrift) and Montelius 1871a and 1871b (*Ny Illusterad Tidning*).

113 On the penetration of Darwinism into Swedish science, see Danielsson 1965 and 1967. On the international status of Darwinism in the 1860s and 1870s, see Ellegård 1957 and 1958 and Vorzimmer 1970 and 1971.

15

General aspects

The half-century between 1820 and 1870 was chiefly distinguished by an endeavour to draw up the main guidelines in chronology. In this way, a basis was also gradually obtained for the surveys of the cultural developments during prehistoric times presented by Thomsen, Magnus Bruzelius, Sven Nilsson, Worsaae and Holmberg. The task had been to classify the archaeological material roughly in chronological order and to gradually try to produce units of time with a somewhat smaller range. I have described the division into the great epochs of the Three-Age System and how the Stone and Bronze Ages were divided into two periods and the Iron Age into three. This was a relatively straightforward course of events, which is fairly clearly distinguished.

The period around 1870 saw a marked change in the development of Scandinavian archaeology and chronological research. No definite limit can be fixed, but it is clear that the latter half of the 1860s and the beginning of the 1870s were, in many respects, a transitional period. The available archaeological material grew rapidly larger and the intensity of research was generally increased. Understanding of the need for greater precision in the type analysis gradually increased and, in parallel with this, the division of the time periods into shorter intervals was accelerated. The quantity of knowledge increased continually and an increasingly large body of accepted facts accumulated, which could be taken for granted in discussion between scholars. As a result, the chains of chronological reasoning and the methods employed became more and more difficult to follow.

With the exception of Worsaae, none of the older generation of antiquarians were professional archaeologists in the true sense of the word. None of them were originally trained for their work. Archaeological research in the early nineteenth century was carried on by a miscellaneous crowd of public officials, lawyers, merchants, artists, teachers, scientists and clergymen. Now, however, a new generation of scholars and museum officials took charge; they had an appropriate university training and possessed other perspectives, aims and means.

For the period before 1870 it is, in the main, not difficult to follow the chronological argumentations. Archaeologists still ascribed a decisive part in the chronological division to observations of the find contexts. My analyses confirm that the evidence of the finds had, in all essentials, provided the basis for the further subdivision of the Iron and Bronze Ages. As *type-forming analogy* is a basic element in all chronological method, it naturally formed an integral part of the methodological equipment of the earliest scientific archaeology. Expanded into the *grouping analogy method* (horizoning and contrasting), type analogy was used at an early date also for generalizing observations of the find contexts. In that way, the *grouping combination method* (horizoning and contrasting) also became one of the commonly used, chronological tools of the early archaeologists. On the whole, find observations were the fixed starting-point for all important chronological advances.

As soon as the internal, chronological stratification of the Iron Age became of topical interest in the mid nineteenth century, *historical sources* came into use, directly and indirectly, in co-operation with the grouping combination method, for the purposes of absolute and relative chronology.

During the 1850s, *stratigraphy* appeared as a method used deliberately and systematically in relative chronology. We first meet with a burial-ground chorology in Vedel's studies in Bornholm at the beginning of the 1870s.

A *grading analogy method* first appeared about 1870. In its actively chronological form, it was preceded, however, by what has here been called a wholly descriptive 'typology', beginning about 1860 in pure prehistory, though much earlier in numismatics.

A *grading combination method* does not seem to have come into systematic use until the 1870s, chiefly in connection with Montelius' periodization of the Bronze Age, which was finally reported in 1885.

We may consequently state that the basic pattern in the method of relative chronology which is still applied today in Scandinavian archaeology as regards the metal ages, *was in principle fully developed even before the end of the nineteenth century*. Most of the methods of archaeological dating discussed in chapter 2 originated and took on their main form during a relatively early period in the history of scientific archaeology. During the same period, the chronological systems for the Bronze and Iron Ages, with which we are still working in the main, were constructed by these methods.

Find analogy by internal, relative, type-frequency comparison was developed late, as a response to a need which was less urgent to the early archaeologists, namely to arrange large, collective finds at dwelling-places in chronological order. This stands out as the only one of the methods of dating discussed here which was developed during the twentieth century; for natural reasons, it has chiefly been used in the field of Stone Age research. However, apart from the new development – that the objects of comparison are frequently numbers – find analogy in the form of frequency seriation and similar procedures nevertheless represents, as a whole, very old chronological principles.

One of these principles is the use in the combination method of the chronological associations of the collective find and the other is the basic idea of the grading analogy method and of evolutionary typology, i.e. the concept of gradual evolution. Owing to the fact that find analogy is based on both these premises simultaneously, it is in no way identical with evolutionary typology. But as find analogy, for example, in the form of frequency seriation, starts, for the actual chronological gradation, to a large extent directly from the basic idea of evolutionary typology, there are nevertheless many points of contact between these methods. The criticism that may be levelled against the starting-point of evolutionary typology – the notion that find grading, according to similarity and dissimilarity, is of reliable, chronological relevance – therefore concerns frequency seriation to an equally great extent, whether it is now expressed in a battleship diagram, in matrix form, as a histogram, in cumulative diagrams, in tables or in some other way.

The difference between then and now, as regards the method of relative chronology, may sometimes appear to be very great. But, basically, this difference relates less to the basic principles of the methods than to the actual technique of application and to the view of the source material's chronological supporting capacity. One line of development has led to an increasingly sophisticated use of statistics, with or without graphic representation. The presence of tables, graphs and diagrams and gradings in virtue of similarity or dissimilarity coefficients or made on the basis of the presence or the frequency principle does not, however, necessarily mean that a modern, chronological principle is being applied. *The starting-points for relative dating are so few that all our chronological manipulations will inevitably be variations on a few original themes.* It is incumbent on each of us – in our own work and in examining the works of other archaeologists – to bear in mind which chronological premiss applies in the individual case and to critically evaluate its chronological supporting capacity, both in principle and in the light of the source material concerned.

When faced with the task of interpreting prehistory in social, economic and cultural terms, the archaeologist has access to an exceptionally abundant and varied, source material. This gives him an opportunity to test new methods and analyse them from fresh viewpoints. In this field, archaeology has also shown an ability to renew itself continuously and to learn from other sciences and ideological schools. For this reason, it is also necessary that an analysis of the development of archaeology as a historical science should take careful account of the general, ideological background of the actual time.

The situation is very different as regards the methods of relative chronology. Archaeology is now a fairly old science, but, in spite of the efforts of generations of archaeologists, the number of dating methods is still amazingly small. The traditional methods as well as the modern, more quantitatively orientated methods are altogether only variations on a few basic themes. The reason for this is that the number of possible dating methods would seem to be proportional to the degree of complexity, as regards dating premises, in the archaeological material. In spite of its richness, the material contains only a few such fundamental dating elements: the analogies which can be made on the basis of the artefacts themselves and their spatial relations. This explains why the number of chronological methods is so small and why new dating methods have *not* been introduced at the same rate as the methodological development of archaeology in general. It is for this reason in particular that ideological impulses from other disciplines are not adequate to give rise to new dating methods. Personally, I doubt whether any archaeological dating method has been created in any other way than, in the main, through deep, empirical experience of a concrete archaeological material.

It is essential to bear these facts in mind in studying the development of the methods of relative chronology. As a method, chronology appears to a very great extent to be a product of empirical research. Just as I doubt that radically new, archaeological methods of dating will be developed in the future, so I equally do not believe that general, ideological influences from other sciences can *primarily* have given rise to such dating methods. They can, like Darwinism, at most, only have accelerated a development which was begun and continued on an infra-scientific basis.

At this point I would like to return to the question of the significance of the typological dating method. The idea that the origin of typology is to be sought in the biological theory of evolution has been so pre-occupying that it has impeded a deeper understanding of the problems associated with the development of the chronological methods. In this work I have maintained that the role played by Darwinism in the emergence of typology was considerably more indirect and secondary than it is usually regarded. The realization that there could be an evolutionary connection between artefacts and other cultural products grew empirically out of observations of find contexts. This was the prerequisite for a theoretical link with Darwinism.

The significance of Darwinism for archaeology is to be found in the fact that it offered a striking parallel to the processes of change in material culture. For this reason, it also came to be regarded as an explanation model. As Darwinism emerged during the formative period of archaeology, when the evolutionary connection between artefact types was becoming clear on purely archaeological evidence, it became involved as a catalyst of this observation. In this way Darwinism doubtlessly stimulated the further study of problems related to the inner evolutionary connection between artefacts.

However, the greatest impact of this analogy with Darwinism was that archaeology became involved in the enormous amount of attention provoked by one of the greatest scientific paradigms of all time. For a quarter of a century archaeology bathed in the glow surrounding Darwinism, a period culminating ideologically in the publication of Montelius' *Typology or the theory of evolution applied to human labour* in 1899. As long as the basic falseness of this analogy went largely unnoticed, the references to Darwinism were a great success; indeed it can certainly be called one of the most brilliant advertising scoops in the history of humanistic science.

As long as Scandinavian typology was firmly rooted empirically, it made important contributions to the methodological development of international prehistoric research. However, during the first half of the twentieth century, both in Scandinavia and elsewhere, evolutionary typology as a dating method was applied in an increasingly mechanical and uncritical way far beyond the scope of its actual possibilities. In this way the typological dating method in many places even came to be regarded as a symbol of an archaeological chronology pursued as an end in itself. Thus the false analogy between cultural and biological evolution became an ideological burden for archaeology.

In my opinion, the scientific importance of Scandinavian typology lies on another, more indirect plane. The typological studies of the 1870s made it necessary for archaeologists to analyse the actual artefacts in a far more painstaking way than they had previously dreamt of. Typology enforced a sorting of the material according to similarities and dissimilarities and this, in its turn, laid the foundations of the archaeological classification method. Thus, for the first time, the type concept was placed at the heart of all archaeological work, regardless of the method used. Scholars became aware of the importance of a more detailed classification. Problems relating to concepts such as natural and artificial types, groups and periods were emphasized. In this respect the work of the Scandinavian typologists was epoch-making methodologically, but more as a side effect than as a direct result of the typological work.

The technique of type classification was of particular significance for the development of the find association method. Thus, the successful development of the find combination method can be largely attributed to the 1870s and 1880s when archaeology took a definite step into the world of more sophisticated type analysis. But the impact of this more detailed type classification was not only on chronology. As it is impossible to execute any archaeological analysis without some sort of basic classification, all other kinds of archaeological study were also affected.

In retrospect it is easy to think that this concentration on the artefactual material dominated for far too long. Nevertheless, it would have been impossible to miss out this stage in the development of archaeology. The wealth of knowledge and experience accumulated in this way is one of the foundation stones which bear up the further development of the subject. Now a great deal of this learning has been lost and replaced by knowledge which today seems more relevant to us. However, it represents a tradition which must to some extent be upheld because it is also important for the development of archaeology as a sociohistorical science.

In my opinion the reputation of the typological dating method has unfairly overshadowed the great impact of the find association method. The technique of making systematic use of observations of find contexts for a more detailed chronology was by far the most important methodological contribution of Scandinavian archaeology in the nineteenth century. It was this, not the evolutionary typology, which laid the foundation for archaeology's development into a modern science.

BIOGRAPHICAL NOTES

Boye, Vilhelm, 1837–96. Danish archaeologist. Graduated in 1856 and subsequently worked at the Museum of Nordic Antiquities. From 1865 he earned his living as a journalist until he was employed, in 1885, at the National Museum. In 1896 he published his famous *Finds from Bronze Age Oak Coffins in Denmark*.

Bruzelius, Magnus, 1786–1855. Swedish archaeologist and clergyman. B. began his career as a physician and chemist. In 1809 he became *docent* (reader) in chemistry at the University of Lund. He also published a French grammar. In the second decade of the century B. devoted himself with great interest to archaeological excavation and to archaeological and historical writing. He also assembled one of the largest collections of antiquities in the country. Ordained as a clergyman in 1819 and in 1824 he became a vicar and later a dean.

Bruzelius, Nils Gustaf, 1826–95. Swedish archaeologist and educationalist. (M. Bruzelius' nephew.) Masters degree in Lund in 1847. B.'s archaeological activity was mainly restricted to the 1850s. In 1855 he became a *docent* (reader) in Nordic archaeology in Lund. Director of the Historical Museum of Lund University 1855–60. From 1860 B. worked as a teacher and head-master at grammar schools.

Danneil, Friedrich, 1783–1868. German prehistorian. D. studied theology and in 1804 he became a grammar school teacher and in 1819 headmaster in Salzwedel, Altmark. D. treated pre-historic material from a principally archaeological point of view.

Engelhardt, Conrad, 1825–81. Danish archaeologist and teacher. Began as an assistant in Thomsen's business firm. From 1851 teacher of English and French in Flensburg in Schleswig. Between 1858 and 1863 he directed the large excavations at the bogs of Thorsbjerg and Nydam. At the outbreak of war with Germany in 1864 E. secretly transported the finds to Copenhagen where he continued his work as a teacher. In 1865 he directed the excavation at Kragehul Bog, and in 1867 he led the investigation at Vimose. From 1867 he worked at the Museum of Nordic Antiquities and directed a number of important excavations. Honorary professor in 1879.

Herbst, Christian Frederik, 1818–1911. Danish numismatist, archaeologist and museum curator. In 1843 engaged by Thomsen as an assistant at the museum in Copenhagen. He carried out a number of important excavations. In 1865 inspector of the Numismatic Collection. In 1866 he became inspector at the Museum of Nordic Antiquities, and in 1865 director of the museum.

Hildebrand, Bror Emil, 1806–84. Swedish numismatist, archaeologist and museum curator. Masters degree at the University of Lund in 1826. Appointed *docent* (reader) in numismatics in 1830. Received a post at the museum in Stockholm in 1832. From 1837 to 1879 H. was King's Custodian of Antiquities. H. received his basic training from his friend C. J. Thomsen in Copenhagen. He introduced the Three-Age System in Lund and Stockholm. He created the Museum of National Antiquities in its modern form. H. had a strong personality which domi-nated antiquarian business in Sweden for a generation.

Hildebrand, Hans, 1842–1913. Swedish archaeologist, numismatist, historian and museum curator. (B. E. Hildebrand's son.) Graduated from Uppsala in 1865. Doctorate in 1866. Took up an appointment at the Royal Academy of Letters History and Antiquities in 1865. Succeeded his father as King's Custodian of Antiquities in 1879, a post which he occupied until 1906. Extensive European study tours in the beginning of the 1860s and the 1870s. General secretary at the international archaeological congress in Stockholm in 1874. H.'s great work *The Prehistoric Peoples of Europe* (1873–80) was the first attempt at a modern summary of prehistory based on a synthesis of archaeology, natural sciences, ethnography, comparative linguistics, comparative religion, literary sources, etc. H.'s *Medieval Sweden* (1879–1903) is still a standard work. H. was a polyhistorian of unusual proportions, and his scholarly production was enormous.

Lindenschmit, Ludwig, 1809–1903. German prehistorian. Worked as a drawing teacher in Mainz. Played an important role in the founding in 1852 of the Central Roman Germanic Museum in Mainz where he was director until his death. Maintained that the ancient Germans constituted the indigenous population of central Europe, and for a long time he refuted the validity of the Three-Age System. Emphasized the significance of the Mediterranean area for the prehistoric metallurgy of central Europe.

Lisch, Friedrich, 1801–83. German prehistorian and historian. Studied history, theology and mathematics. From 1827 appointment at the Gymnasium Friedricianum in Schwerin. Became Archivist of the Grand Duchy. Organized the large collections of antiquities at Schwerin. Received the honorary title of doctor in 1848.

Montelius, Oscar, 1843–1921. Swedish archaeologist and museum curator. Graduated from Uppsala University in 1868. Doctorate in 1869. Had a post as the Museum of National Antiquities in Stockholm from 1868 to 1907. King's Custodian of National Antiquities from 1907–13. Received the title of professor in 1888.

M. undertook extensive study tours abroad. He was deeply fascinated by the chronological problems of the metal ages all over Europe and the Mediterranean area. His production in this field was huge and innovative. M. was primarily an empiricist with an unusual ability to perceive causal relationships and pick out pertinent information. His research, his extrovert nature and his linguistic skill made M. one of the cnetral figures in European archaeology.

Müller, Sophus, 1846–1934. Danish archaeologist and museum curator. Graduated in classical philology in 1871. Until 1876 he earned his living as a teacher while also assisting Worsaae at the Museum of Nordic Antiquities. In 1878 M. received employment at the museum and in 1892 he became director of the prehistoric department. Undertook extensive study tours in Europe in the 1870s.

M. was a versatile and productive archaeologist and also an excellent synthesist. For its time, his general work on the prehistory of Denmark (*Vor Oldtid*, 1897) was a masterpiece which still has something to offer the reader. By virtue of his capacity and strong personality he dominated Danish archaeology for a very long time. Alongside Montelius, M. was the leading Nordic archaeologist of his time.

Nilsson, Sven, 1787–1883. Swedish zoologist and prehistorian. Masters degree in Lund in 1811. Became *docent* (reader) in natural history in 1812 and in 1818 he graduated from the University of Lund in medicine. In 1818 he took up a post at the University Museum of Natural History. Professor of Natural History from 1832 to 1856. As a zoologist N. was a pioneer in the faunistic and paleozoological spheres. As a prehistorian N. was the first person to apply systematically ethnographic analyses to the study of archaeological material.

Steenstrup, Japetus, 1813–907. Danish zoologist. In 1845 he became Professor of Zoology in Copenhagen. Pioneering studies of the octopus. His botanical work on the bogs of Zealand was of great significance for archaeologists. With Worsaae and the geologist Forchhammer he formed part of the scholarly committee for research into the Danish shell middens. S. minted the expression 'kitchen middens'.

Thomsen, Christian Jürgensen, 1788–1865. Danish archaeologist and numismatist. Son of a wealthy business man in Copenhagen, T. was economically independent. He received a good school education but never pursued university studies. Worked in his father's firm from an early age, cultivating at the same time his antiquarian interests. Took over the business in 1833 and did not terminate it until 1840.

At an early age T. began to assemble coins, paintings, copperplates and antiquities. In 1816 he was appointed secretary of the Royal Commission for the Preservation of Antiquities and was given complete freedom to organize its collections. In 1827 he himself became a member of the commission. In 1832 T. became inspector at the Numismatic Collection and in 1846 its director. In 1838 he became inspector of the Museum of Nordic Antiquities and in 1849 its director. In 1839 he became inspector of the Art Museum and the Collection of Paintings.

T. is said to have had a kind and pleasant personality. He was a skilled administrator and an important innovator for the museum collections in Copenhagen. His written scientific production was restricted, but he effectively expressed his scientific ambitions through the museum medium and through his extensive personal contacts at home and abroad.

Vedel, Emil, 1824–1909. Danish archaeologist and civil servant. Graduated in law in 1846. As a county prefect on the island of Bornholm from 1866 to 1871, he carried out extensive surveys of burials from the early Iron Age. He excavated a very great number of these graves and quickly published his results in a manner which was innovative for its time.

Worsaae, Jens Jacob Asmussen, 1821–86. Danish archaeologist and museum curator. W. carried out excavations while still a boy and came into contact with Thomsen at the museum. At the age of 17 he published his first scholarly archaeological study.

Alongside his work as Thomsen's unsalaried assistant, W. made a living from other work, while at the same time pursuing law studies. From 1844 he devoted himself entirely to his antiquarian work. In 1847 he became inspector of ancient monument preservation in Denmark, and he became director of the Museum of Nordic Antiquities and of the Ethnographic Museum in 1865. From 1874 to 1877 W. was minister for cultural affairs. In 1854 he was awarded the title of professor.

W. was president of the international archaeological congresses at Copenhagen (1869), Bologna (1871) and Stockholm (1874). In 1846 and 1847 he made extensive study tours on the Continent and the British Isles. W. was an independent scholar, critical as well as constructive, and had an unusual talent for interpreting cultural relations from a general, international perspective. W. was also a skilled administrator, and a charming extrovert man of the world with close connections to the royal family.

REFERENCES

ABBREVIATIONS

Aarbøger   Aarbøger for nordisk Oldkyndighed og Historie. Copenhagen.
Annaler   Annaler for nordisk Oldkyndighed og Historie. Copenhagen.
ATA   Antikvariskt Topografiska Arkivet. Stockholm.
ATS   Antiqvarisk Tidskrift för Sverige. Stockholm.
KVHAA Handl.   Kungl Vitterhets Historie och Antikvitets Akademiens handlingar.
                Stockholm.
MLUHM   Meddelanden från Lunds Universitets Historiska Museum. Lund.
Månadsblad   Kongl Vitterhets Historie och Antiqvitets Akademiens Månadsblad.
                Stockholm.
Oversigt   Oversigt over det Kongelige Danske Videnskabernes Selskabs Forhandlinger
                og dets Medlemmers Arbeider. Copenhagen.
SFT   Svenska Fornminnesföreningens Tidskrift. Stockholm.

Åberg, A., 1966. Oscar Montelius, arkeologiens Linné. *Industria* 1966: 11. Stockholm, pp. 86–7,
    114, 116, 118.
Åberg, N., 1924. *Den nordiska folkvandringstidens kronologi*. Stockholm.
    1929. Typologie (Typologische Methode). *Reallexikon der Vorgeschichte*, herausg. v. Max
Ebert, Bd 13. Berlin, pp. 508–16.
    1943. *Oscar Montelius som forskara. Till 100-årsminnet av Montelii födelse den 9 sept. 1843*.
    KVHAA Handl. 57.
Almgren, B., 1967. Das Entwicklungsprinzip in der Archäologie – eine Kritik. *Tor*, 11, 1965–6,
    pp. 15–38. Also in Swedish Udviklingsproblemer. Nordisk Sommeruniversitet 1958.
    København 1959, pp. 110–24.
Almgren, O., 1921. Oscar Montelius. *Historisk Tidskrift* 1921. Stockholm, pp. 303–8.
Andersen, P. S., 1960. *Rudolf Keyser. Embetsmann og historiker*. Bergen.
Andersson, N. J., 1869. Darwinismen. *Framtiden* 2, 1869, pp. 673–96.
    1871. Charles Darwin, 1–5. *Ny illustrerad tidning* 1871, häfte 16, 17, 19, 24, 26 (s. 121f., 150,
    185f., 202f.). Stockholm.
Arbman, H., 1954. Hallands forntid. In *Hallands historia från äldsta tider till freden i Brömsebro
    1645*. Halmstad, pp. 1–207.
    1969. Arkeologi i Norden. In Moberg, C. A., *Introduktion till arkeologi*. Stockholm, pp. 33–5.
Arne, T. J., 1908. Hans Hildebrand som förhistoriker. *Ord och Bild* 17, 1908: 8, pp. 215–18.
    1922. Oscar Montelius och hans instatser i svensk fornforskning. *Nordisk tidskrift* 1922, pp.
    5–22.
    1934. Hans Hildebrand som förhistoriker. *Fornvännen* 29, 1934, pp. 317–26.
Bachman, M.-L., 1969. *Studier i Kungl. Vitterhets Historie och Antikvitets Akademiens historia*.
    KVHAA Handl., Hist. ser. 14. Stockholm.
Becker, C. J., 1948. *Mosefundne Lerkar fra yngre Stenalder. Studier over Tragtbaegerkulturen i
    Danmark*. København.
Bibby, G., 1957. *The testimony of the spade*.

Binford, L. R., 1972. Post-Pleistocene adaptations. In *An archaeological perspective*. New York, pp. 421–49. Also in: *New perspectives in archaeology*. Ed. by S. R. Binford and L. R. Binford. Chicago 1968, pp. 313–41.

Blainville, H. M. D. de, 1816. *Prodrome d'une nouvelle distribution du règne animal*. Paris.

Böhner, K., 1981. Ludwig Lindenschmit and the Three Age system. In *Towards a history of archaeology*. Being the papers read at the first conference on the history of archaeology in Aarhus, 29 August–2 September 1978. Thames and Hudson, London. pp. 120–6.

Boye, V., 1858. Begravelser fra Steen- og Bronze-Alderen, undersögte og beskrevne. *Annaler* 1858, pp. 200–15.

    1860. Bidrag til Kundskab om den aeldre Jernalder i Danmark. *Annaler* 1860, pp. 26–61.

    1866. Gravhøie fra Broncealderen. *Aarbøger* 1866, pp. 215–32.

    1869. Ättehögar i Södra Halland. *Hallands Fornminnes-Förenings Årsskrift* 1, 1868–72, pp. 75–118.

Brenner, E., 1731. *Thesaurus nummorun sueo-gothicorum* (2nd edn). Holmiae (Stockholm).

Brøgger, A. E., 1925. *Det norske folk i oldtiden*. Oslo.

Brøndsted, J., 1958. *Danmarks Oldtid. II. Bronzealderen*. København.

Brown, H. A., 1889. On some small highly specialized forms of stone implements, found in Asia, North Africa and Europe. *The Journal of the anthropological institute of Great Britain and Ireland* 18. London, pp. 134–9.

Bruzelius, M., 1816. Beskrifning på några Antiquiteter af koppar, funna i Skytts härad, Malnöhus län. *Iduna* 6, pp. 45–70.

    1816–18. *Specimen Antiquitatum Borealium*, 1–2 (1816), 3 (1818). Lund.

    1817. Nordiska Fornlemningar. *Iduna* 7, pp. 189–205.

    1820. Nordiska Fornlemningar. *Iduna* 8, pp. 89–105.

    1822. Nordiska Fornlemningar från Skåne. *Iduna* 9, pp. 285–333.

    1823. Om Nordiska Sten-Antiquiteternas ålder och bruk. *Physiographiska Sällskapets Årsberättelse, aflemnad af dess Secreterare, den 6 Maj 1823*. Lund, pp. 53–5.

Bruzelius, N. G., 1853. *Svenska Fornlemningar, aftecknade och beskrifna*, I. Skåne. Lund.

    1854a. Beskrifning öfwer några snäckhögar och ruiner efter boningar, belägna på Kullaberg. *Oversigt* 1854, pp. 197–204.

    1854b. Beskrifning om åtskilliga i Skåne och södra Halland belägna fornlemningar, hvilka under åren 1853 och 1854 blifvit undersökta. *Annaler* 1854, pp. 339–57.

    1857. Beskrifning om fornlemningar i Skåne. *Antiquarisk Tidsskrift* 1855–7, pp. 72–87.

    1860. *Beskrifning om åtskilliga i Skåne och södra Halland belägna fornlemningar, hvilka under åren 1853 och 1854 blifvit undersökta*. Lund. Also as *Beskrifning öfver Svenska Fornlemningar jemte en kort framställning af den äldre Jernåldern i norra och mellersta Europa*. Lund 1860.

Christie, J., 1842a. Antiquarisk-historisk Skitse af Augvaldsnaes. *Urda* 2, pp. 322–47.

    1842b. Beretninger om Fund af Oldsager i Norge, isaer i Bergens Stift. *Urda* 2, pp. 387–407.

Clarke, D. L., 1968. *Analytical archaeology*. London.

Daniel, G., 1943. *The three ages*. Cambridge.

    1950. *A hundred years of archaeology*. London.

    1967. *The origins and growth of archaeology*. Harmondsworth.

    1975. *A hundred and fifty years of archaeology*. Duckworth.

Danielsson, U., 1965. Darwinismens inträngande i Sverige. *Lychnos* 1963–4, pp. 157–210.

    1967. Darwinismens inträngande i Sverige. II. *Lychnos* 1965–6, pp. 261–334.

Danneil, J. F., 1836. Generalbericht über Ausgrabungen in der Umgegend von Salzwedel. *Neue Mitteilungen aus dem Gebiet historisch-antiquarischer Forschungen* 2: 3/4, 1836.

Darwin, C., 1868. *The variation of animals and plants under domestication*. London.

    1871a. *Om arternas uppkomst genom naturligt urval eller de bäst utrustade rasernas bestånd i kampen för tillvaron*. Stockholm.

    1871b. *The descent of man and selection in relation to sex I, II*. London.

    1872. *Människans härledning och könsurvalet*. Stockholm.

Eggers, H. J., 1959. *Einführung in die Vorgeschichte.* München.

Ellegård, A., 1957. The Drawinian theory and the argument from design. *Lychnos* 1956, pp. 173–92.

1958. *Darwin and the general reader. The reception of Darwin's theory of evolution in the British periodical press, 1859–1872.* Göteborg.

Engelhardt, C. 1858. Om Sønder-Brarup Fundet. *Slesvigske Provindsialefterretninger,* I Bind, 3die Hefte. 19 pages.

1863. *Thorsbjerg Mosefund. Beskrivelse af de Oldsager som i Aarene 1858–61 ere udgravede af Thorsbjerg Mose ved Sønder-Brarup i Angel; et samlet Fund, henhørende til den aeldre Jernalder og bevaret i Den Kongelige Samling af Nordiske Oldsager i Flensborg.* Kjöbenhavn.

1865. *Nydam Mosefund, 1859–1863.* Kjöbenhavn.

1866. Kragehul Mosefund. *Aarbøger* 1866, pp. 157–72.

1867a. *Kragehul Mosefund, 1751–1865. Et Overgangsfund mellem den aeldre Jernalder og Mellem-Jernalderen.* Kjöbenhavn.

1867b. Om Vimose-Fundet. *Aarbøger* 1867, pp. 233–57.

1868. *Museet for de nordiske Oldsager. En kort Ledetraad for de besøgende.* Anden udgave. Kjøbenhavn.

1869. *Vimose Fundet.* Kjøbenhavn.

1873. Valløby Fundet. *Aarbøger* 1873, pp. 285–320.

1875. Klassisk Industri og Kulturs Betydning for Norden i Oldtiden. *Aarbøger* 1875, pp. 1–94.

Eriksson, G., 1969. *Romantikens världsbild speglad i 1800-talets svenska vetenskap.* Stockholm.

Evans, J., 1864. *The Coins of the Ancient Britons.* London.

1872. *The Ancient Bronze Implements, Weapons and Ornaments of Great Britain and Ireland.* London.

Filip, J., 1966. Bronzezeit. *Enzyklopädisches Handbuch zur Ur- und Frühgeschichte Europas, I.* Prag, pp. 170–1.

Flit i fält (1967). Flit i fält 1963–1966. Specialupplaga av *Finskt museum* 1967 tillägnad det XII Nordiska arkeologmötet i Helsingfors den 4–9 juni 1967. Helsingfors.

Forchhammer, G. and Steenstrup, J., 1848. Beretning om Leire-Egnens geognostiske Forhold. *Oversigt* 1848, pp. 62–75.

Furumark, A., 1950. Några metod- och principfrågor inom arkeologien. In *Från filosofiens och forskningens fält. Nya rön inom skilda vetenskaper.* Uppsala, pp. 168–214.

Gjessing, G., 1946. To metodiske problemer. *Viking* 10, pp. 123–60.

Gorodzov, V. A., 1933. The typological method in archaeology. *American Anthropologist* 35, 1933, pp. 95–102.

Gräslund, B., 1974. Relativ datering. Om kronologisk metod i nordisk arkeologi. *Tor* 16, 1974. Uppsala.

1976a. Relative chronology. Dating Methods in Scandinavian Archaeology. *Norwegian Archaeological Review,* 9: 2, 1976, pp. 69–83.

1976b. Reply to Comments on Relative Chronology. *Norwegian Archaeological Review* 9: 2, 1976, pp. 111–26.

1981. The background to C. J. Thomsen's Three-Age System. In *Towards a History of Archaeology. Being the papers read at the first Conference on the History of Archaeology in Aarhus, 29 August–2 September 1978.* Ed. by G. Daniel. Thames & Hudson. London, pp. 45–50.

Haeckel, E. 1868. *Ueber die Entstehung und den Stammbaum des Menschengeschlechts.* Sammlung gemeinverständlicher wissenschaftlicher Vorträge, herausgegeben von Rud. Virchow und Fr. v. Holtzendorff. III Serie, Herf 52–53. Berlin.

1873. *Natürliche Schöpfungsgeschichte. Gemeinverständliche wissenschaftliche Vorträge über die Entwicklungslehre im allgemeinen und diejenige von Darwin, Goethe und Lamarck im besonderen.* 4. Aufl. Berlin.

Hallenberg, J., 1800. *Collectio nummorum cuficorum, quos aere expressos, addita eorum interpretatione, subjunctoque alphabeto cufico.* Stockholm.
  1819. *Berättelse om ett forntids Romerskt Metallkärl funnet i Westmanland år 1818.* Stockholm.
Heizer, R. F., 1962. The background of Thomsen's Three-Age System. In *Technology and Culture. The International Quarterly of the Society for the History of Technology.* Summer 1962. Detroit, pp. 25–266.
Herbst, C. F., 1865. Varpelev Fundet. *Annaler* 1861, pp. 305–22.
  1866. Om Opdagelsen af den aeldre Jernalder. Oplysninger i Anledning af J. A. A. Worsaaes foranstaaende Bemaerkninger. *Aarbøger* 1866, pp. 360–76.
  1867. Ogsaa en Slutningsbemaerkning. *Aarbøger* 1867, p. 262.
Hermansen, V., 1934. C. J. Thomsens første Museumsordning. Et Bidrag til Tredelingens Historie. *Aarbøger* 1934, pp. 99–122.
Hildebrand, B., 1934. Bror Emil Hildebrand, hans liv och gärning. Föredrag i Svenska Fornminnesföreningen den 4 oktober 1934. *Fornvännen* 29, 1934, pp. 257–316.
  1937–8. *C. J. Thomsen och hans lärda förbindelser i Sverige 1816–1837. Bidrag till den nordiska forn- och hävdaforskningens historia I–II.* KVHAA Handl. 44.
  1943. Hans Hildebrand. Till hundraårsminnet. *Scandia, Tidskrift för historisk forskning* 1943: 1, pp. 95–157.
Hildebrand, B. E., 1829. *Numismata Anglo-Saxonica Musei Academiae Lundensis ordinata & descripta.* Lundae (Lund).
  1842. Utlåtande öfver märkvärdigare Jordfynd, som blifvit Kongl. Maj:t och Kronan hembjudna. Stockholm. *Aftryck ur K. Witterhets, Historie och Antiqvitets Akademiens Handlingar,* pp. 329–57.
  1844. *Anteckningar ur Kongl. Witterhets, Historie och Antiqvitets Akademiens Dagbok samt om de under Akademiens inseende ställda Kongl. Samlingarna för år 1843.* Stockholm.
  1846. *Anglosachsiska mynt i svenska Kongl. Myntkabinettet, funna i Sveriges jord.* Stockholm.
  1869. Till hvilken tid och hvilket folk böra de Svenska Hällristningarne hänföras? *ATS* 2, 1869, pp. 417–32.
  1884. *Lefnadsteckning* (Autobiography). Manuscript in the possession of Professor Karl-Gustaf Hildebrand, Uppsala.
Hildebrand, H., 1866. *Scenska folket under hednatiden.* Stockholm.
  1867. Stenåldern i forntiden. *Svensk Literatur-tidskrift* 3,1867, pp. 261–7.
  1869a. Den äldre jernåldern i Norrland. *ATS* 2, pp. 221–332.
  1869b. [Review of] Lubbock, Menniskans urtillstånd eller den förhistoriska tiden belyst genom fornlemningarne och seder och bruk hos nutidens vildar. Övers. av C. W. Paijkullu. I:sta häftet. *Svensk tidskrift för literatur* 1869, p. 130.
  1869c. Geologi. [Review of] Erdmann, Bidrag till kännedomen om Sveriges Qvartära Bildningar, Stockholm 1868. *Svensk tidskrift för literatur* 1869, pp. 57–64.
  1870. Fölhagen-fyndet. *ATS* 3, pp. 51–112.
  1871a. *Les fibules de l'âge du bronze groupées. Aperçu provisoire tiré des préparations pour un ouvrage sur la civilisation de l'âge du bronze.* Stockholm.
  1871b. [Review of] Scriptores rerum svecicarum medii aevi. Tom: III. Sectio posterior. Upsaliae. *Svensk tidskrift för literatur* 1871, pp. 549–51.
  1872a. *Svenska folket under hedna tiden.* 2nd edn, Stockholm.
  1872b. De arkeologiska perioderna. *Månadsblad* 1, jan. 1872, pp. 2–10.
  1872–80. Studier i jämförande fornforskning. I. Bidrag till spännets historia. *ATS* 4, 1872–80, pp. 1–263.
  1873a. *Den vetenskapliga fornforskningen, hennes uppgift, behof och rätt.* Stockholm.
  1873b. Ormhufvud-ringarne från äldre jernåldern. *Månadsblad* 14, febr. 1873, pp. 24–30. *Månadsblad* 15, mars 1873, pp. 36–41.
  1873c. Sur les fibules de l'âge du bronze. *Congrès international d'anthropologie et d'archéologie préhistoriques. Compte rendu de la session à Bologne 1871.* Bologne, pp. 214–16.

1873–80. *De förhistoriska folken i Europa. En handbok i jämförande fornkunskap.* Stockholm.

1876a. Den anthropologisk-arkeologiska kongressens sammanträde i Stockholm. *Månadsblad* 33, sept. 1874, pp. 119–34.

1876b. Sur les commencements de l'âge du fer en Europe. *Congrès international d'anthropologie et d'archéologie préhistoriques. Compte rendu de la 7e session. Stockholm. 1874.* Stockholm, pp. 592–601.

1877. Fyndet från Ödeshög, 1–2. *Månadsblad* 67–70, juli–okt. 1877, pp. 501–9, 521–9.

1878. Jernåldern på Gotland. 1–2. *Månadsblad* 79–84, juli–dec. 1878, pp. 702–10, 733–57.

1879. Jernåldern på Gotland. 3–4. *Månadsblad* 87–8, mars–apr. och 95–6, nov.–dec. 1879, pp. 49–60, 163–80.

1881. Statens Historiska Museum och K. Myntkabinettet. *ATS* 6: 6, pp. 1–62.

1882. Från äldre tider. Kulturvetenskapliga och historiska studier. *Menniskan i den förhistoriska tiden.* Stockholm, pp. 114–203.

1884. Bror Emil Hildebrand. *Månadsblad* 151–3, juli–sept. 1884, pp. 97–134.

1886. Zur Geschichte des Dreiperiodensystems. *Zeitschrift für Ethnologie* 18, 1886, pp. 357–67.

1887. Treperiodsystemets uppkomst. *Månadsblad* 175–7, juli–sept. 1886, pp. 128–39.

Hindenburg, T., 1869. Bemaerkninger i Anledning af den internationale archaeologiske Kongres i Kjøbenhavn fra 27de August til 3die September 1869. *Aarbøger* 1869, pp. 369–97.

Hofsten, N. von. 1922. Från Cuvier till Darwin. Ett blad ur den jämförande anatomiens historia. *Nordisk tidskrift* 1922, pp. 389–411.

1928. *Skapelsetro och uralstringshypoteser före Darwin.* Uppsala Universitets Årsskrift 1928. Program 2. Uppsala.

Holmberg, A. E. 1854. *Nordbon under hednatiden. Populär framställning af våra förfäders äldsta kultur.* Stockholm.

Huxley, Th. H., 1873. *Critiques and addresses.* London.

Jacob Friesen, G., 1967. *Bronzezeitliche Lanzenspitzen Norddeutschlands und Skandinaviens.* Hildesheim.

Jacob-Friesen, K. G., 1928. *Grundfragen der Urgeschichtsforschung. Stand und Kritik der Forschung über Rassen, Völker und Kulturen in Urgeschichtlicher Zeit.* Hannover.

Jankuhn, H., 1936a. Zur Deutung des Moorfundes von Thorsbjerg. *Forschungen und Fortschritte* 12, Berlin, pp. 202.

1936b. Die religionsgeschichtliche Bedeutung des Thorsberger Fundes. Forschungen und Fortschritte 12, Berlin, pp. 365–7.

Johannsen, W., 1917. *Falska analogier med hänsyn till likhet, släktskap, arv, tradition och utveckling.* Stockholm.

Keller, F., 1858. (Untitled article on the La Tène finds.) *Mitteilungen der antiquarischen Gesellschaft in Zürich* 12: 3, 1858, pp. 116, 151ff. Zürich.

Keyser, R., 1836–7. Beskrivelse over tvende Fund paa Ringerige i Norge af Oldsager fra Hedenskabets sidste Periode. *Annaler* 1836–7, pp. 142–59.

1839. Om Nordmaendenes Herkomst og Folke-Slaegtskab. *Samlinger til det norske Folks Sprog og Historie* II. Christiania, pp. 263–462.

Klejn, L., 1982. *Archaeological typology.* BAR Intern. Ser. 153. Oxford.

Klindt-Jensen, O., 1975. *A History of Scandinavian Archaeology.* London.

Kock, A., 1917. Hans Hildebrand. Kungl. *Svenska Vetenskapsakademiens Årsbok för år 1917.* Uppsala, pp. 273–92.

Kossinna, G., 1913a. Oscar Montelius zum 31. März 1913. *Mannus* 5, pp. 105–7.

1913b. Zur älteren Bronzezeit Mitteleuropas IV. *Mannus* 5, pp. 160–70.

1922. Oscar Montelius. *Mannus* 13, pp. 309–35.

Kristiansen, K., 1978. Dansk arkeologi – fortid og fremtid. In *Fortid og nutid,* 27: 3, 1978, pp. 279ff.

Lewenhaupt, E., 1922. Oscar Montelius. *Rig, Tidskrift utgiven av föreningen för svensk kulturhistoria* 5, 1922, pp. 2–16.

Liljegren, J. G., 1830. Strödda anteckningar om fynd i Svensk Jord, med dertill hörande Förteckning. *Kongl. Vitterhets Historie och Antiquitets Academiens Handlingar*, 30. Stockholm, pp. 153–278.

Liljegren, J. G. and Hildebrand, B. E. 1832. Sverige I. Efterretningar om fundne nordiske Oldsager samt om større Mindesmaerker fra Oldtiden og Middelalderen. *Nordisk Tidsskrift for Oldkyndighed* I, pp. 225–40.

Lindqvist, S., 1922. Oscar Montelius som fornforskare. *Ymer* 41, 1921, pp. 209–23.

Lisch, F., 1837. *Friderico-Francisceum oder Grossherzogliche Alterthümsammlung aus der alt- germanischen u. slawischen Zeit Mecklenburgs Ludwigslust.* Leipzig.

1857a. Kegelgrab von Dabel Nr. I. *Jahrbücher Schwerin* 22, pp. 279–87.

1857b. Kegelgrab von Mühlengeez. *Jahrbücher Schwerin* 22, pp. 287–8.

1858. Kegelgrab von Dabel Nr. 3. *Jahrbücher Schwerin* 23, pp. 279–84.

1859. Kegelgrab von Brunsdorf. *Jahrbücher Schwerin* 24, pp. 267–9.

Lorange, A., 1874. Om Spor af romersk Kultur i Norges aeldre Jernalder. *Forhandlinger i Videnskabs-Selskabet i Christiania Aar 1873*, pp. 184–236, Christiania.

Lubbock, J., 1865. *Pre-historic times, as illustrated by ancient remains, and manners and customs of modern savages.* London.

1872. *Pre-historic times, as illustrated by ancient remains, and the manners and customs of modern savages.* 3rd edn, London.

Lundqvist, M., 1943. *Bibliotheca Monteliana. Katalog över Oscar Montelius boksamling i Kungl. Vitterhets Historie och Antiquitets Akademiens bibliotek.* KVHAA Handl. 57.

Lyell, C., 1863. *The geological evidences of the antiquity of man with remarks on theories of the origin of species by variation.* London.

1867–8. *Principles of geology or the modern changes of the earth and inhabitants considered as illustrative of geology.* I–II, 10th edn, London.

1871. *The student's elements of geology.* London.

Mackeprang, M., 1929. Fra Nationalmuseets barndom. *Fra Nationalmuseets Arbejdsmark 1929.* København, pp. 5–14.

Madsen, A. P., 1872. *Afbildninger of danske Oldsager og Mondesmaerker. Broncealderen. Suiter.* Kjøbenhavn.

1876. *Afbildninger af danske Oldsager og Mindesmaerker. Broncealderen II. Samlede fund.* Kjøbenhavn.

Montelius, O., 1869a. *Från Jernåldern.* Stockholm.

1869b. Halländska fornsaker från Hednatiden. *Hallands Formminnes- Förenings Årsskrift* I, 1868–72, pp. 49–74.

1870. De denska mossfynden och deras betydelse för den nordiska fornforskningen. *Framtiden* 3, 1870, pp. 199–216.

1871a. Sigurdsristningarne i Södermanland. *Ny Illustrerad Tidning* 1871, No. 14. Stockholm, pp. 110–11.

1871b. Bilder från historiska museet. *Ny Illustrerad Tidning* 1871, No. 25. Stockholm, pp. 194–5.

1872a. *Sveriges forntid. Försök till framställning af den svenska fornforskningens resultat. Atlas. Svenska fornsaker, I. Stenåldern och bronsåldern.* Stockholm.

1872b. *Statens Historiska Museum. Kort beskrifning till vägledning för besökande.* Stockholm.

1872c. Halländska fornsaker från Hednatiden. 2. Halländska fornsaker i andra samlingar än Statens Historiska Museum. *Hallands Formminnes-Förenings Årsskrift* I. 1868–72, pp. 121–205.

1872d. Romerska och byzantinska mynt funna i Sverige. *Månadsblad* 4, apr. 1872, pp. 55–61, 73–6, 81–4.

1872–3. Bronsåldern i norra och mellersta Sverige. *ATS* 3: 2–4, pp. 173–433.

1873a. Sur les époques de l'âge du bronze en Suède. *Congrès international d'anthropologie et d'archéologie préhistoriques. Compte rendu de la cinquième session à Bologne 1871.* Bologne, pp. 288–94.

1873b. Ett fynd af frankiska mynt i Sverige. *Månadsblad* 23, nov. 1873, pp. 169–72.

1873c. Om de ovala spännbucklorna. *Månadsblad* 24, dec. 1873, pp. 177–94.

1874a. Angelsaksiska mynt funna i Småland. *Månadsblad* 27, mars 1874, pp. 43–6.

1874b. Om förhållandet mellan den äldre och den yngre bronsåldern i Norden. *Forhandlingerne ved de skandinaviske Naturforskeres 11te Møde i Kjøbenhavn fra den 3die til den 9de Juli 1873.* Kjøbenhavn, pp. 641–5.

1875. L'âge du bronze en Suède. *Congrès international d'anthropologie et d'archéologie préhistoriques. Compte rendu de la 4e session, Copenhague 1869.* Copenhague, pp. 249–55.

1876a. Sur l'âge du bronze en Suède. *Congrès international d'anthropologie & d'archéologie préhistoriques. Compte rendu de la 7e session. Stockholm, 1874.* Stockholm, pp. 488–512.

1876b. Sur les poignées des épées et des poignards en bronze. *Congrès international d'anthropologie & d'archéologie préhistoriques. Compte rendu de la 7e session, Stockholm, 1874,* pp. 888–923.

1877a. Sur les celts en bronze. *Congrès international d'anthropologie et d'archéologie préhistoriques. Huitième session à Budapest 1876.* Budapest, pp. 304–8.

1877b. Två bronsåldersfynd från Kareby socken i Inlands södra härad. *Bidrag till kännedom om Göteborgs och Bohusläns fornminnen och historia* 3–4. Stockholm, pp. 271–320.

1878. *Om tidsbestämning inom bronsåldern, med särskildt afseende, på Skandinavien.* Manuscript. ATA.

1880. Bohuslänska fornsaker från hednatiden, 3. *Bidrag till kännedom om Göteborgs och Bohusläns fornminnen och historia* 5. Stockholm, pp. 30–57.

1880–2. Spännen från bronsåldern och ur dem närmast utvecklade former. Typologisk studie. *ATS* 6: 3, pp. 1–194.

1881a. Om den nordiska bronsålderns ornamentik och dess betydelse för frågan om periodens indelning. *Månadsblad* 110–13, febr.–maj 1881, pp. 17–71.

1881b. Minnen från bronsålderns slut i Nordern. *Månadsblad* 103–4, juli–aug. 1880, pp. 97–123.

1882. Ett fynd från vår bronsålders äldsta tid. *Månadsblad* 105–8, sept.–dec. 1880, pp. 129–58.

1883. 'Brandpletter' i Östergötland. *Månadsblad* 130–2, okt.–dec. 1882, pp. 181–5.

1884a. Den förhistoriske fornforskarens metod och material. *ATS* 8: 3, pp. 1–28.

1884b. Bror Emil Hildebrand. *Ny Illustrerad Tidning* 1884, No. 3, Stockholm, pp. 331–2.

1885a. *Om tidsbestämning inom bronsåldern med särskild hänsyn till Skandinavien.* Kongl. Vitterhets Historie och Antiqvitets Akademien. Handlingar 30, ny följd, 10. Stockholm.

1885b. Sur la chronologie de l'âge du bronze, spécialement dans la Scandinavie. *Matériaux pour l'histoire primitive de l'homme.* 3me Série, Tome II, Mars 1885. Paris, pp. 3–8.

1887. Runornas ålder i Norden. *SFT* 6, pp. 236–70.

1892. Öfversigt öfver den nordiska forntidens perioder, intill kristendomens införande. *SFT* 8, pp. 127–63.

1895–7. Den nordiska jernålderns kronologi, 1–3. *SFT* 9, pp. 155–274, *SFT* 10, pp. 55–130.

1899. Typologien eller utvecklingsläran tillämpad på det menskliga arbetet. *SFT* 10: 3, pp. 237–68.

1900. *Die Chronologie der ältesten Bronzezeit in Nord-Deutschland und Skandinavien.* Braunschweig.

1903. *Die typologische Methode. Die älteren Kulturperioden im Orient und in Europa, I.* Stockholm.

1905. Det nordiska treperiodsystemet. En historik. *SFT* 12, pp. 185–211.

1915. *Bror Emil Hildebrand. Minnesteckning.* K. Svenska Vetenskapsakademiens Lefnadstechningar 5. Stockholm.

1919. Med Oscar Montelius genom tre sekler. I–VI. *Aftonbladet* 1919. (12.1, 19.1, 16.2, 16.3, 6.4, 27.4). Stockholm.

1986. *Dating in the Bronze Age with special reference to Scandinavia.* With an introduction by Bo Gräslund, Stockholm.

Müller, S., 1874. En Tidsadskillelse mellem Fundene fra den aeldre Jernalder i Danmark. *Aarbøger* 1874, pp. 335–92.
   1880. Dyreornamentiken i Norden. *Aarbøger* 1880, pp. 185–405.
   1884. Mindre bidrag til den forhistoriske Archaeologis methode. *Aarbøger* 1884. København.
Nerman, B., 1921. Oscar Montelius. *Upplands fornminnesförenings tidskrift* 26. Uppsala, pp. 289–96.
Neumann, J., 1842. Gravurnerne i det Bergenske Museum. *Urda* 2, pp. 1–11.
Niklasson, N., 1955. När och av vem präglades uttrycket mesolitikum? *Fornvännen* 50, 1955, pp. 46–9.
Nilsson, S., 1838–43. *Skandinaviska Nordens Ur-invånare, ett försök i komparativa ethnografien och ett bidrag till menniskoslägtets utvecklings-historia*. Lund.
   1855. *Skandinavisk Fauna. 4. Fiskarna*. Lund.
Nordén, A., 1921. Minnesruna över Oscar Montelius. *Norrköpings Tidningar* 5.11.1921.
Nordman, C. A., 1915. Den förhistoriska arkeologins metod. I–II. *Nya Argus* 1915, Nr 19–20. Helsingfors, pp. 176–8, 184–5.
Obermaier, H., 1927. Mesolithikum. *Reallexikon der Vorgeschichte*, herausg. v. Max Ebert, Bd 8. Berlin, pp. 154–5.
Ørsnes, M., 1969. *Sønderjyske og fynske Mosefund. Bind I. Thorsbjerg Mosefund*, af Conrad Engelhardt. With preface by Mogens Ørsnes. København.
   1970b. *Sønderjyske og fynske Mosefund. Bind III. Kragehul og Vimosefundene*, af Conrad Engelhardt. With preface by Mogens Ørsnes. København.
Padberg, W., 1953. Evolutionsgeschehen und typologische Methode. *Jahresschrift für Mitteldeutsche Vorgeschichte* 37. Halle (Saale), pp. 19–48.
Petersen, C. J., 1938. *Stenalder, Broncealder, Jernalder. Bidrag til nordisk Archaeologis Litteraerhistorie 1776–1865*. København.
Petrie, W. N. F., 1901. Diospolis Parva. The cemeteries of Abadiyeh and Hu 1898–9. *The Egypt Exploration Fund. Memoirs* 20. London.
Piggott, S., 1960. Prehistory and evolutionary theory. Evolution after Darwin. *The university of Chicago centennial. II. The evolution of man. Man, culture and society*. Chicago, pp. 85–97.
Quatrefages, A. de, 1870. *Charles Darwin et ses précurseurs français. Étude sur le transformisme*. Paris.
Quennerstedt, A., 1871. Om Darwinismen. *Svensk tidskrift för literatur* 1871, pp. 479–528.
Retzius, G., 1873. *Om de äldsta spåren af menniskans tillvaro*. Ur vår tids forskning 5. Stockholm.
   1933. *Biografiska anteckningar och minnen. I*. Uppsala.
   1948. *Biografiska anteckningar och minnen. II*. Uppsala.
Rodden, J., 1981. The development of the Three Age System: Archaeology's first paradigm. In *Towards a History of Archaeology. Being the papers read at the first conference on the History of Archaeology in Aarhus, 29 Aug.–2 Sept. 1978*. Ed. by G. Daniel. Thames & Hudson, London, pp. 51–68.
Rosén, J., 1966. Arkeologen och hans hjälpmedel. I *Den svenska historien. I. Forntid, vikingatid och tidig medeltid till 1319*. Stockholm, pp. 38–43.
Rydbeck, O., 1943a. Oscar Montelius. *Sydsvenska Dagbladet* 8.9.1943.
   1943b. Dan arkeologiska forskningen och Historiska museet vid Lunds universitet under tvåhundra år, 1735–1937. *MLUHM* 1943, pp. 165–440.
Rydh, H., 1937. *Oscar Montelius. En vägrödjare genom årtusenden*. Stockholm.
Rygh, O., 1869. Om den aeldre Jernalder i Norge. *Aarbøger* 1869, pp. 149–84.
Sacken, E. von, 1868. *Das Grabfeld von Hallstatt in Oberösterreich und dessen Alterthümer*. Wien.
Salin, B., 1922. *Minnesteckning över Oscar Montelius*. KVHAA Handl. 34: 1.
Schetelig, H., 1914. Arkeologiske Tidsbestemmelser av aeldre norske Runeindskrifter. *Norges Indskrifter med de aeldre Runer*. III. 1914–24. Christiania, pp. 1–76.
Schröder, J. H., 1849. *De moneta anglo-saxonica ejusque variis typis. Observationes nonnullae*. Upsaliae (Uppsala).

Seger, H., 1930. Die Anfänge des Dreiperioden-Systems. *Schumacher Festschrift. Zum 70. Geburtstag Karl Schumachers*. Mainz, pp. 3–7.

Sernander, R., 1922. Oscar Montelius och den svenska naturforskningen. *Nordisk Tidskrift* 1922, pp. 52–63.

Sorterup, J. B., 1846. *Kort Udsigt over Museet for Nordiske Oldsager*. Kjøbenhavn.

Steenstrup, J., 1848. Om Dannelsestiden for visse Lag af Østers- og Musling-Skaller i Danmark. *Oversigt* 1848, pp. 7–12.

1851a. Beretning om geologisk-antiquariske Undersögelser ved Isefiord og i Jylland. *Oversigt* 1851, pp. 1–31.

1851b. Anden Beretning om geologisk-antiquariske Undersögelser. Sommeren 1851. *Oversigt* 1851, pp. 179–222.

1853. Beretning om Fremgangen i de forenede Forskninger for at oplyse Denmarks aeldste Natur- og Culturforhold. *Oversigt* 1853, pp. 14–31.

1854. Fortsaettelse af geologisk-antiquariske Undersøgelser. *Oversigt* 1854, pp. 191–7, 204–7.

1855a. Bidrag til Danmarks forhistoriske Fauna. *Oversigt* 1855, pp. 1–20, 52.

1855b. Udbyttet af 1854 i Jylland foretagne geologisk-antiquariske undersøgelser. *Oversigt* 1855, pp. 131–2.

1860. Om Hr. Professor Worsaaes Tvedeling af Steenalderen. *Oversigt* 1859. 23 pages.

1862a. Imod Hr. Professor Worsaaes Tvedeling af Steenalderen, et Bidrag til Forstaaelsen af Steenalderens Kultur her i Norden. *Oversigt* 1861. 74 pages.

1862b. Et Blik paa Natur- og Oldforskningens Forstudier til Besvarelsen af Spørgsmaalet om Menneskeslaegtens tidligste Optraeden i Europa. (Første Afsnit.) Saerskilt Aftryk af *Indbydelsesskrift til Reformationsfesten ved Khøbenhavns Universitet 1862*. Kjøbenhavn. 42 pages.

Stenberger, M., 1964. *Det forntida Sverige*. Uppsala.

Thomsen, C. J., 1831. *Om nordiske Oldsager og deres Opbevaring*. 13 pages. Kjøbenhavn.

1831–4. *Fortegnelse over Georg Friedrich Timms udmaerkede Mynt- og Medaillesamling. Deel I–III*. Kjøbenhavn.

1932a. Untitled article. *Nordisk Tidskrift for Oldkyndighed* I, pp. 420–1.

1832b. Kortfattet Udsigt over nordiske Steen-Oldsager fra den hedenske Tid, med kobberstukne Afbildninger. *Nordisk Tidskrift for Oldkyndighed* I, pp. 421–39.

1832c. Danmark. I Efterretninger om fundne nordiske Oldsager samt om større Mindesmaerker fra Oldtiden og Middelalderen. *Nordisk Tidsskfirt for Oldkyndighed* I, pp. 174–224.

1833. Antiquariske Efterretninger. Danmark. *Nordisk Tidsskrift for Oldkyndighed* 2, pp. 169–92, 247–76.

1836. *Ledetraad til Nordisk Oldkyndighed*. Kjøbenhavn, pp. 27–90.

1848. *A Guide to Northern Archaeology*. London.

1855. Om Guldbracteaterne og Bracteaternes tidligste Brug som Mynt. *Annaler* 1885, pp. 265–347.

1858. Sendschreiben an die erste Section der Versammlung deutscher Alterthums- und Geschichtsforscher zu Berlin. *Korrespondenzblatt des Gesamtvereines der Deutschen Geschichts- und Alterthumsvereine* VI. Berlin, pp. 114–15.

1864. Självbiografiska anteckningar. Nationalmuseets archiv, Köpenhamn.

Thordeman, B., 1934. Hans Hildebrand som medeltidsforskare. Anförande i Svenska Fornminnesföreningen den 4 okt. 1934. *Fornvännen* 29, 1934, pp. 327–36.

Tischler, O., 1885. Über die Gliederung der La-Tène-Periode. *Correspoondenz-Blatt der deutschen Gesellschaft für Anthropologie, Ethnologie und Urgeschichte* 16. München.

Torell, O., 1876. Sur les traces les plus anciennes de l'existence de l'homme en Suède. *Congrès international d'anthropologie & d'archéologie préhistorique. Compte rendu de la 7ᵉ session, Stockholm, 1874. Appendice*. Stockholm, pp. 861–76. Cf. pp. 16, 144.

Tornberg, C. J., 1848. *Numi cufici regii numophylacii holmiensis, quos omnes in terra Sueciae repertos digessit et interpretatus est.* Upsaliae (Uppsala).

Torstendahl, R., 1964. *Källkritik och vetenskapssyn i svensk historisk forskning 1820–1920.* Uppsala.

Undset, I., 1881. *Jernalderens Begyndelse i Nord-Europa. En Studie i sammenlignende forhistorisk Archaeologi.* Kristiania.

Vedel, E., 1870. Om de bornholmske Brandpletter. Begravelser fra den aeldre Jernalder. *Aarbøger* 1870, pp. 1–110.

1872. Den aeldre Jernalders Begravelser paa Bornholm. Med Tillaeg til foranstaaende Meddelelser om den aeldre Jernalders begravelser paa Bornholm. *Aarbøger* 1872, pp. 1–84.

1873. *Undersøgelser angaaende den aeldre Jernalder paa Bornholm.* Kjøbenhavn.

1878. Nyere Undersøgelser angaaende Jernalderen paa Bornholm. *Aarbøger* 1878, pp. 73–258.

Vedel Simonsen, L. S., 1813. *Udsigt over Nationalhistoriens aeldste og maerkeligste Perioder,* I. København.

Vorzimmer, P. J., 1970. *Charles Darwin: the years of controversy. The origin of species and its critics 1859–1882.* Philadelphia.

1971. Darwin's 'Lamarckism' and the 'Flat-Fish controversy' (1863–1871). *Lychnos* 1969–70, pp. 121–70.

Weibull, L., 1923. Det arkeologiska treperiodsystemet. Dess uppkomst och giltighet. *Historisk Tidskrift för Skåneland* 5, 1914–23. Lund, pp. 247–66.

Westropp, H. M., 1872. *Pre-historic phases; or, introductory essays on pre-historic archaeology.* London.

Wiberg, C. F., 1861. *Bidrag till kännedom om Grekers och Romares förbindelse med Norden och om de nordiska handelsvägarne.* Gefle.

1867. *De klassiska folkens förbindelse med Norden och inflytande på dess civilisation. Ett bidrag till Östersjöländernas kultur historia.* Stockholm.

Worsaae, J. J. A., 1841. Undersögelser af Gravhöie i Danmark. *Annaler* 1840–1, pp. 137–63.

1843. *Danmarks Oldtid oplyst ved Oldsager og Gravhøye.* Kjøbenhavn.

1846a. *Blekingske Mindesmaerker fra Hedenhold betragtede i deres Forhold til de övrige skandinaviske og europaeiske Oldtidsminder.* Kjøbenhavn.

1846b. Den nationale Oldkyndighed i Tydskland: Reisebemaerkinger. *Annaler* 1846, pp. 116–50.

1846c. *Die nationale Alterthumskunde in Deutschland.* Kopenhagen.

1847. Jernalderens Begyndelse i Danmark, oplyst gjennem Gravfund. *Annaler* 1847, pp. 376–87.

1849a. *The Primeval Antiquities of Denmark.* London.

1849b. Fund af romerske Oldsager i Danmark. *Annaler* 1849, pp. 391–9.

1852a. Beretning om et maerkeligt Fund fra Meilgaardsegnen imellen Randers og Grenaa. *Antiquarisk Tidsskrift* 1849–51, pp. 98–100.

1852b. Antiqvarisk Iagttagelser fra en Reise i Normandiet og Bretagne. *Oversigt* 1852, pp. 218–36.

1854. *Afbildninger fra Det Kongelige Museum for Nordiske Oldsager i Kjøbenhavn.* Kjøbenhavn.

1858. Om Jernalderen i Danmark. I Anledning af et Fund Oldsager i en Mose ved Brarup i Angel. *Oversigt* 1857.

1859. *Nordiske Oldsager i det Kongelige Museum i Kjøbenhavn.*

1860a. Om En ny Deling af Steen- og Broncealderen, og om Et Maerkeligt Fund fra den aeldre Steenalder ved Engestofte paa Laaland. *Oversigt* 1859, 37 pages.

1860b. Om nogle i Maribo Sø, fornemmelig i Egnen af Engestofte, nylig opdagede Spor af Paele, og om talrige ved disse fundne Flintsager fra den aeldre Steenalder. *Oversigt* 1859, pp. 117–29.

1862a. Om tvedelingen af Steenalderen. *Oversigt* 1861, 64 pages.

1862b. Gjensvar paa Hr. Prof. Steenstrups yderligere Bemaerkninger imod Tvedelingen af Steenalderen. *Oversigt* 1861, 24 pages.

1865. *Om Slesvigs eller Sønderjyllands Oldtidsminder*. Kjøbenhavn.

1866a. Conferentsraaderne C. C. Rafn's og C. J. Thomsen's Fortjenster af Oldskriftselskabet og af Oltidsvidenskaben i det Hele. Mindeord. *Aarbøger* 1866, pp. 107–17.

1866b. Om Opdagelsen af den aeldre Jernalder. Bemaerkninger til C. F. Herbst's Beskrivelse af 'Varpelev-Fundet'. *Aarbøger* 1866, pp. 349–60.

1867. Slutningsbemaerkninger om Opdagelsen af den aeldre Jernalder. *Aarbøger* 1867, pp. 257–62.

1877. Om Bevaringen af de faedrelandske Oldsager og Mindesmaerker i Danmark. *Aarbøger* 1877, pp. 1–54.

1881. *Nordens Forhistorie efter samtidige Mindesmaerker*. Kjøbenhavn.

1884. Om Ordningen af arkaeologisk-historicke Museer i og udenfor Norden. *Nordisk tidskrift* 1884, pp. 162–82.

1934. *En Oldgranskeres Erindringer*. Udgivet ved V. Hermansen. København.

INDEX

Åberg, N., 101
Almgren, B., 100

Becker, C. J., 38
Blainville, H. M. D. de, 98, 110
Boucher de Perthes, J., 38
Boye, V., 41–2, 46, 92, 118
Bronze Age, 3, 17, 20–3, 27,
    30–1, 40–6, 56–8, 60, 70–85,
    91–7, 113
Brown, J. A., 38
Bruzelius, M., 14, 31–3, 113, 118
Bruzelius, N. G., 14, 40–3, 46–7,
    56, 66, 93, 113, 118
Büsching, J. G. G., 26

Caesar, Julius, 48
Carlyle, A. C., 38
chorology, 59
chronological methods, concepts
    and terms, 5–11
chronology, absolute, 48–9, 54
Christy, H., 106
coins, 26, 49, 51, 54, 66–8
combination method, 7–9, 22–3,
    38, 43–4, 50, 54–5, 58–9,
    63–4, 76, 81, 89, 91, 114, 117
Cuvier, G., 30, 110

Danneil, J. F., 18–19, 118
Darwin, C., 101, 106
Darwinism, 101–12, 116

Engelhardt, C., 50, 54, 66, 93,
    118
Evans, Sir J., 100

Forchhammer, J. G., 35

Gorodzov, 98, 110

Herbst, C. G., 49–51, 118
Hildebrand, B. E., 14, 16, 19,
    20, 38, 48–9, 66–8, 93,
    98–100, 108–9, 118
Hildebrand, H., 13–16, 32, 57,
    60, 62, 65–8, 88, 91–3,
    95–102, 104–11, 118–19
historical dating, 54, 114
Holmberg, A. E., 113
Hylander, S., 66, 117

Iron Age, 3, 17, 20–3, 30–1,
    48–68, 113; pre-Roman,
    48–55, 62–5; Roman, 56–60;
    middle, 51–5, 63

Keyser, R., 20, 48
Klindt-Jensen, O., 1

Lartet, E., 106
Lindenschmidt, L., 16, 19, 119
Lisch, F., 18–19, 118
Lyell, Sir C., 11, 30, 106

Madsen, A. P., 93
mesolithic, concept of, 34–8;
    term, 38
Montelius, O., 1, 3, 10, 13–14,
    42, 56, 65–8, 70–3, 76–81,
    83–98, 100–11, 114, 116, 119
Müller, S., 14, 62–6, 68, 72, 83,
    88, 119

national collections, importance
    of, 14–16
neolithic, concept of, 34–8; term,
    38
Nilsson, S., 2, 14, 28, 30, 113,
    119
numismatics, 99–101

Padberg, 30
Petrie, Sir W. Flinders, 100

quantitative methods, 10–11,
    114–15

Retzius, A. J., 32
Retzius, G., 106

Sacken. E. von, 56
Schröder, J. H., 23–4
Sjöborg, N., 32
Sorterup, J. B., 43, 93
Steenstrup, J., 34–5, 37–8, 119
Stolpe, H., 14
Stone Age, 17–23, 31–8, 113–14
stratigraphy, stratigraphic
    dating, 10, 40–4, 81, 83, 114

Tacitus, 48
Thomsen, C. J., 1, 2, 13–32,
    48–9, 56, 66, 93, 113, 120
Three-Age system, 13, 17–31, 111
Tischler, O., 57
Torell, O., 38
Tornberg, C. J., 68
type, term, 97–8
typology (grading type analogy),
    5–7, 9, 26–7, 60, 64, 81,
    86–108, 114–17; descriptive,
    44–5, 59–60, 107–8; origin of,
    96–112; term, 97–9

Vedel, E., 57–60, 108, 120
Vedel Simonsen, L. S., 17

Westropp, H. H., 38
Worsaae, J. J. A., 2, 13–16, 20,
    25, 27, 30, 34–51, 54, 60,
    65–6, 92–3, 108–9, 113, 120

www.ingramcontent.com/pod-product-compliance
Ingram Content Group UK Ltd.
Pitfield, Milton Keynes, MK11 3LW, UK
UKHW030902150625
459647UK00021B/2661